Contemporary Thai

Contemporary Thai

By Wongvipa Devahastin na Ayudhya
with Jane Marsden Doughty
Photography by Luca Invernizzi Tettoni

PERIPLUS

Published by Periplus Editions (HK) Ltd.
Copyright © 2000 Periplus Editions (HK) Ltd.

ISBN 962-593-828-1
Printed in Singapore

Editor: Kim Inglis
Author: Jane Doughty Marsden
Design: m(in)d, London

Distributed by:
North America, Latin America and Europe
Tuttle Publishing, Distribution Center,
Airport Industrial Park, 364 Innovation Drive,
North Clarendon, VT 05759.
tel (802) 773 8930; fax (802) 773 6993

Asia Pacific
Berkeley Books Pte Ltd, 5 Little Road #08-01,
Singapore 536983.
tel (65) 280 3320; fax (65) 280 6290

Japan
Tuttle Publishing, RK Building, 2nd Floor,
2-13-10 Shimo-Meguro, Meguro-Ku, Tokyo 153.
tel (813) 5437 0171; fax (813) 5437 0755

Indonesia
PT Java Books Indonesia, Jl Kelapa Gading Kirana,
Blok A14 No 17, Jakarta 14240.
tel (62) 21 451 5351; fax (62) 21 453 4987

Previous page: Adding warmth to a contemporary home are this lamp base and vase in strong lines and earthy colours designed by Eakrit Praditsuwana of Earth & Fire, Bangkok.

Right: One night in Bangkok. *Bai-sri* and bencharong are a sophisticated combination at the Peninsula Hotel. The ancient floral decorative arts of *bai-sri* and *phoum* (by Sakul Intakul studio) complement this stylish dinner set from Naga House, Bangkok.

Overleaf: Traditional festival cloth lanterns enhance the rustic feel of Chairat Kamonorathep's open-air *sala* in Chiang Mai.

Contents

8 The New Thai Style

10 Contemporary Thai Interiors

30 The Art of Thai Accents

48 Dramatic Table Settings

68 Thai Fabrics Old and New

92 New Trends in Bamboo and Rattan

110 Earthenware and Ceramics

130 Romantic Thai Nights

142 Acknowledgments

The New Thai Style

One evening late in the 20th century, movie director Roman Polanski arrived at the Cannes Film Festival with his stunning young actress wife Emmanuelle Seigner. Her radiance was rivalled only by the single and singularly large luminescent pearl suspended like a sun-kissed dewdrop round her neck. Polanski was later to say that "the mixture of traditional handicraft and sophisticated elegance" of the Thai jewel was superb.

Of the same Bangkok-based boutique which made the one-off piece for Polanski—Lotus Arts de Vivre—fashion designer Kenzo Takada has noted its "plainness, modernity and discreet references to the past". One can imagine the admiration of guests at Kenzo's Phuket villa when champagne is presented in an ice-bucket made of car tyres and sterling silver or wine in a rattan holder once used to store hill-tribesmen's seeds.

Thai style lies at the confluence of time-honoured handicrafts and contemporary tastes. It is the tension between Eastern ornateness and Western relevance; between palatial splendour and pared-down simplicity.

One only has to gaze at the kaleidoscopic colours, glittering and gilded finials and myriad decorative devices at Bangkok's Grand Palace to realise that traditional Thai style is one of Asia's most flamboyant and also one most permeable to outside influences. This is probably just as well, because the current global emphasis on clarity and simplicity in interior design has required significant streamlining by artisans traditionally employed to present the most intricate and elaborate treasures to the temple or palace. Methods and materials once reserved for royalty such as gold-leaf stencilling, lacquerware and the finest silks and celadons are now being utilised with an eye for their modern form and function. Presentation counts but not at the expense of practicality. Thus, a heavily carved and gilded altar table inspires a clean-lined, versatile side console by Thai furniture designer Ou Baholyodhin, whose clients include Donna Karan and Madonna. Modern aesthetics also apply; hence the neutral colour palette for silk ordered from Jim Thompson by UK Prime Minister Tony Blair for No. 10 Downing Street.

It is also useful to remember that furniture was not customarily found in Thai homes apart from those of the upper classes. Indeed, while meticulously crafted, village objects had practical designs fashioned from local, sustainable materials. In a reverse take, the new Thai style elevates the simple to satisfy the sophisticated. Bamboo and rattan furniture, upholstered in the latest washable, rotatable natural fabrics, is now as presentable in the parlour as it was on the patio. Tribal *khit* and *yan lipao* baskets, encouraged by mentors like Queen Sirikit's Support Foundation, are now elegant vases, lamp shades, napkin holders and trinket boxes. Contemporary Thai style incorporates both ends of the

Above: Gold-leaf work on this maroon lacquered panel at the Lanna Spa, Regent Resort Chiang Mai, depicts the tree under which the Buddha was meditating when he attained enlightenment. The puppet is in Burmese style. Stencilling and spa designed by Lek Bunnag, Bangkok.

Opposite Middle Right: Suite dreams are made of silken walls and homespun cotton bed linen at this suite in the Peninsula Hotel, Bangkok.

Opposite Far Right: Derived from Pwo Karen hill-tribe baskets used to store pumpkin seeds, the design of this wicker wine holder from Sop Moei Arts, Chiang Mai, took nine months to perfect.

local design spectrum, mixing colours, patterns and forms to create new styles suitable for modern living.

Certain basic tenets, however, remain unchanged. Thai style has always revered the natural and the supernatural; many of its expressions reflect both. A simple lotus, when folded and placed in a stem vase or grown in a glazed water jar, becomes both an exquisite floral decoration and an offering to Buddha. A path flickering with candles in tiny terracotta bowls *(tien prateep)* or a pool studded with floating candles are not only fabulously festive uses of fire but also forms of worship.

While not all of us can live in a rarefied wooden enclave on a Bangkok *klong,* a converted rice barn in the Chiang Mai mountains or an idyllic seaside retreat off Krabi, a rustic ambience can be achieved through the use of basic elements in the home. Natural fibres such as cotton, hemp, linen and silk and quick-growing, renewable resources such as mangowood, water hyacinth and bamboo are experiencing a renaissance, just as recycled pieces have gained new respectability. A feeling of *sabai* (well-being) is as close as your hand-hewn teak coffee-table or the stack of cinnamon sticks in the corner pot.

Just as the West has become wistful about its increasing removal from natural beauty, so too is it suffering from a lack of the spiritual solace which has always been central to Thai style. This may be as simple as lighting incense to evoke a meditative mood or as complex as appreciating a dinner-set design derived from ancient temple murals.

While a sense of fun *(sanuk)* is intrinsic to a culture which exults in the mystical and the magical, there is still a seriousness associated with honouring certain traditions. Most followers of Thai style, such as singer Elaine Paige who was in Phuket recently to source a Buddha image for her home, are aware of the need to treat such objects with respect (and not place them in the bedroom or bathroom, for example).

Another factor affecting Thai style is the fragility of the very handicrafts on which it relies. There is a feel-good factor in knowing that the purchase of a fruit basket shaped like a Pwo Karen rice-thresher, a jute mat woven by Narathiwat Muslims or a television cupboard consisting of old Buddhist scripture-chest panels contributes directly to the survival of its producers.

King Chulalongkorn, who ordered no less than 14 bencharong tea sets in different hues for each of his 77 children, might have been bemused by the minimalism of Emmanuelle Seigner's necklace. But his commitment to modernisation as a means of preserving Thai ways would surely have caused him to embrace the latest design accents in the ongoing dialogue between his nation and its global partners.

Contemporary
Thai Interiors

An openness to overseas influences anchored to an age-old attention to detail defines the new direction in Thai-style homes. Whether it's the sublimely subtle suggestion of a series of exposed pillars in a living pavilion or the full-blown fantasy of a penthouse palace, Thai interiors merge modern lifestyle with master craftsmanship. Preciousness is passé. Chair covers, for example, are made of durable materials and rotated according to occasion, season and mood. Recycled wood and renewable resources are the rage, as old methods combine with old materials to create new forms. Thai style is not only attainable, it is sustainable.

A House in Wood

Threefold desires to display a museum-standard collection of Asian art and antiques, conserve northern Thai architectural forms and entertain on a grand scale led to this warm, rich fusion of Eastern and Western styles.

The owner, an international banking consultant, commissioned US architect David De Long to design what is now his home for half of every year. De Long imposed a Frank Lloyd Wright linearity on the traditionally Thai series of linked pavilions raised on pillars (to maximise ventilation and avoid flooding and snakes). His brief was to incorporate as many traditional Thai architectural forms as possible. "The traditional forms are exceptionally beautiful and rarely used any more except in temples," the owner says. "My great fear is that they will be lost, which would be tragic indeed, as age-old design can be adapted to accommodate modern living. Much of any culture is expressed in architecture; to abandon traditional forms is to diminish one's culture."

In keeping with Buddhist custom, the predominantly teak house recalls the days when even royal palaces were built of wood, more durable building materials being reserved for religious structures. A triumph of proportions, the design boasts lofty ceilings and floor-to-ceiling windows which ensure that air-conditioning is kept to a minimum. Externally the vernacular prominent roof was left devoid of the usual buffalo-horn-shaped crests *(galae)* for a contemporary smoothness, while the interior is an admirable mix of modern and traditional Thai styles overlaid with a Wrightian rigidity.

Vestibules act as breathing spaces as well as display areas for artefacts. "Some of the crates I showed up with at airports around Asia left more than one of the check-in staff gasping," recalls the owner. In the living pavilion, an 1850s Mandalay gable and Cambodian standing Buddha complement furniture upholstered in Thai cotton designed by De Long. Another highlight of the owner's collection is a 19th-century, red and gold manuscript cabinet which combines both Lanna and Chinese styles—"a real museum piece". In the dining room are two early-19th-century illustrated Lanna manuscripts, probably the greatest treasure in the house. "It portrays the Lanna people as a fun-loving joyous tribe," says the owner. "The text is written in the Lanna script, which is now virtually dead."

Previous page: High life. Frank Lloyd Wright-inspired furniture is juxtaposed with a 19th-century, miniature architectural model for a temple. The 600-sq-m grand salon with its sweeping, 11 m-high teak ceiling is the second largest residential living room built in the last 100 years and designed by a major architect. The Johnson house designed by Frank Lloyd Wright in the '30s is the largest.

Opposite: Flanked by two rare illustrated manuscripts, an imposing spirit house, carved like a palace, underlines the formality of the huge dining-room. Gold Thai silk panels are a suitably rich backdrop for other artefacts from Kalimantan, Pakistan, India, Malaysia and China.

Left: One of the few air-conditioned rooms in the house, the library features a wood panel guarded by life-like 19th-century Burmese gong carriers which conceals the unsightly modern cooling apparatus. The Chinese-influenced teak desk made in Chiang Mai and custom-made leather chesterfield sofa signal a departure from the geometric designer furniture of the living and dining rooms.

Precious Mettle

It takes a certain audacity to live with lashings of lacquer. For the guest rooms of his northern-style home in Chiang Mai, Dusit Salakshana has put this age-old Thai decorative device to flamboyant use.

Gold and silver leaves respectively were applied to panels of wood on the walls of the Gold and Silver Rooms, lending them a lovely luminescence difficult to achieve by other methods. Reconstructed from old doors, the panels were first covered with a black lacquer base which took several weeks to dry properly. Even the door knobs were colour-matched in the painstaking process.

Lacquer adorns not only the wooden walls and cabinet in the Gold Room, but also the teakwood bed which shines a rich ebony. Canopied, cushioned and covered in homespun Thai cotton, the bed was designed by Teerapoj Kaenchan who was also responsible for the interior.

Several Burmese pieces are a nod to the importance of Myanmar in northern Thai culture. A chest—reconstructed from panels from a Burmese temple—supports Burmese gong carriers at the entrance to the house. Framed Burmese scriptures enhance the formality of the Gold Room. A British bed from colonial Burma, also covered with Thai cotton, occupies the Silver Room.

In this luxurious case, as in the royal chambers of old, lacquer and metallic leaf have been applied lavishly and lovingly with stunning results.

Opposite and Above: Old architectural ink drawings of Lanna temples and a series of traditional zodiac signs in pewter are highlights in the Silver Room. The pewter-topped celadon containers are from Living Space, Chiang Mai.

Left: Burmese gong carriers offer a whimsical welcome. Chiang-Mai architect Chulathat Kitibutr incorporated slanting walls and the traditional flame-motif *galae* (crests) typical of Lanna homes in his design.

Above: The dining room. Chairs are upholstered in silk from Jim Thompson, while the side console is constructed from panels taken from an old northern Thai building.

Right: Regal room. The lacquered teak bed by interior designer Teerapoj Kaenchan has the inward-turning legs typical of much Thai furniture. The gilded bedside cabinet is from Gong Dee Gallery, Chiang Mai, while the lacquered boxes and lamp are from Living Space, Chiang Mai.

Height of Taste

Given its gloriously gilded surfaces and magnificent murals, it is appropriate that this penthouse suite is closer to heaven than most. Drawing on classical temple motifs and the exquisite art of *lai kham* (gold-leaf stencilling), designer M.R. Powari Suchiva fulfilled the owner's brief to create a sumptuous palace in the sky.

These lofty pretensions are certainly justified. At 5,000 sq m, the Thai section of the uptown Bangkok apartment can cater to a court of 1,500. (European and Indian sections, also solely for entertaining rather than residential purposes, occupy other floors.)

A panoply of *devas* (temple divinities), reminiscent of those guarding ancient royal chambers, greets guests in the lift lobby. These gold-leaf and gold-paint wall murals by Gong Dee Gallery's Vichit Chaiwong continue in the drawing-room where they segue into more sensual and surreal forms, indicative of a modern approach to an art once reserved for Buddhist temples. Chaiwong took more than one year to complete all the murals, many of which were inspired by 1950s' master painter Angkarn Kalayanapongsa.

The interplay of contemporary and classical is matched by a daring dynamic between European and Eastern furnishings and accents. An antique Thai palace screen, positioned for *feng shui* purposes to encourage energy to flow slowly through to the drawing room, is a backdrop for two bulky Victorian armchairs. In the dining-room, the custom-made, 30-seat table is close to the floor as per Thai tradition but cleverly conceals a leg recess to permit Western-style sitting.

In the ceilings, handcarved teak panels with silver leaf finish in floral motifs, similar to the *ham yon* wooden lintels placed above the doorways of northern houses to protect against evil spirits, lure the eye upwards. No expense has been spared to ensure that these expansive premises, like their owner, exude power and privilege.

Above: Celestial sight. Painstakingly painted classical Thai *devas* (guardian divinities) in the entrance lobby herald the heavenly visions—and view—beyond the heavily carved and gilded teak doors.

Opposite: Screen play. A gilded reproduction Ayudhaya screen, originally used as a dressing mirror, catches the eye immediately upon entry to the apartment. It rests on an antique Ayudhaya sitting platform.

Opposite: Inner sanctum. Occidental meets Oriental in a provocative pairing of two Victorian armchairs with a reproduction Laotian bronze frog drum from Art Resources, Bangkok.

Right Top: A Ratanakosin-style Buddhist scripture cabinet near a modern charcoal-grey sofa is a study in contrasts. The gilded lacquer screen is from Gong Dee Gallery. A coconut coir mat and a bronze bird-leg side table from Art Resources, Bangkok, are other eclectic elements.

Right Below: Ornate Italian Neo-Rococo chairs upholstered in Thai silk complement the gilded delicate carvings on a Ratanakosin-era manuscript cabinet. Lamp bases fashioned from Burmese-style *kinnara* and *kinnari* (half-bird, half human figures from Buddhist cosmology) in lacquered wood continue the classic Thai theme. A bencharong stem vase is on the table.

Right and Below: High table. The much-used dining room is dominated by a sunken teak table with a cleverly concealed leg recess. The gold Thai silk *mon kwang* (triangular cushions) are from Jim Thompson. Sunset shimmers on the Chao Phraya River 36 storeys below.

Far Below: Doorways shaped like those in a Thai temple lead from the dining room to a glass-and-chrome staircase which seems to float above the town of Nonthaburi, about 20km north of Bangkok.

Contemporary Furniture

The furniture, as well as the architecture, of today's affluent Southeast Asia can be divided broadly into two movements: one with direct references to vernacular styles; the other revealing a more abstracted language built on lines, edges and planes. Such is the division among the home furnishings at Jim Thompson which include both an exclusive collection by Ou Baholyodhin and a more recognisably Thai line by Prinya.

Madonna, Karl Lagerfeld and Joseph are all clients of the award-winning Ou whose work is in The Conran Shops in London, Paris and Tokyo; Corso Como 10 in Milan; Troy in New York; Abode in Tokyo; Ipuri in Hamburg and his own studio in London's East End. His success indicates a global demand for furnishings which, while Asian, blend seamlessly with other pieces and styles in the home.

Within the idiomatic movement, the Thai furniture connoisseur would further distinguish regional styles. Perhaps the most popular is that emanating from the former capital of the Lanna Kingdom, Chiang Mai, the base for much of this new furniture-making industry.

Northern nuances, reviving Lanna Kingdom techniques and styles in distinctly modern applications, reflect the new confidence of Chiang Mai artisans, once overshadowed by their Bangkok counterparts.

Above: A teak dining table at Chairat Kamonorathep's home glitters with *lai kham* work by Gong Dee Gallery, Chiang Mai, which also produced the bedside cabinet, *right.*

Right: Something old, something new. The slick angles of a teak scroll altar table by Ou Baholyodhin accentuate the coarse texture of this 17th-century Mon Buddha triptych from the Kaw Gun Cave.

Below Left: Chinese forms influence these side tables designed by Ou Baholyodhin.

Below Right: This teakwood cabinet from AKA, Bangkok, has the tapered form typical of traditional northern-style furniture and houses, yet has a timeless quality suitable for modern interiors.

Opposite: Architect and AKA furniture designer Eakrit Praditsuwana calls his signature style "neo-romantic functionalism". All of his pieces salute Thailand's rich heritage, and he is particularly influenced by the work at Wat Prathat Lampang Luang. Hand-woven, easy-care fabrics such as cotton in neutral colours, shown here, complement contemporary shapes in teak. The screen print on mulberry paper inspired by a temple mural and the Earth & Fire ceramic tea set are also designed by Eakrit.

The lowdown on the latest teak coffee-tables by Prinya for Jim Thompson:

Above: Paired with Thai silk cushions from Jim Thompson, this table is perfect for relaxing in the Oriental style.

Right: This version has distinctively Thai curved legs.

Far Right: Wicker insets— *à la* the current mode of finishing antique daybeds from China—are light and fashionable.

Above: Gin and tonic, anyone? The deckchair, once *de rigueur* on the verandahs of expatriate homes in Southeast Asia, gains a new lease of life with upholstery in thick Thai cotton. An ornate Dutch colonial lamp adds to the nostalgic feel. A Lanna vase and offering trays rest on a manuscript cabinet—reconstructed and decorated with Lanna-style lacquered patterns.

Second-hand Splendour

Recycled pieces—especially given today's concern over diminishing natural resources such as wood—are aesthetically pleasing, supremely functional and politically correct. Whole villages in Thailand, such as Hang Dong just outside of Chiang Mai, are now devoted to turning temple brackets into table bases and manuscript cabinets into cupboards—with the same levels of craftsmanship and labour that went into making the original objects. Indeed, it is precisely the demand for recycled pieces that keeps many of these traditional crafts (and craftsmen) alive.

Humour and homage combine in some of the best recycled elements: a soldier's helmet does duty as a lamp stand; a reconstructed xylophone-like *song mon*, traditionally used at funerals, summons hotel guests to dinner; a bedside-lamp base in a honeymoon suite utilises wood from a temple pillar; cabinets which once held precious scriptures now conceal television sets.

In the open-air reception *sala* at Baan Suan restaurant, Chiang Mai (*pictured right*) four scroll-shaped eave brackets from an old temple make an attractive table base. Other recycled elements include a gilded Lanna-style temple gable, now an eye-catching wall feature, and a cupboard constructed from panels of old lacquered manuscript cabinets.

Modern incarnations of utilitarian or even religious items are limited only by the imagination of the eventual owner.

Above: The open-air reception *sala* at Baan Suan Restaurant, Chiang Mai.

Left: A pair of comfortable art deco-inspired armchairs assembled from old teak complement a console of old manuscript cabinet pieces at Baan Suan.

Far Left: Homespun cotton cushions add warmth to this family room. The chest, which serves as both coffee-table and storage space, is from recycled wood, as is the mirror frame.

The Art of
Thai Accents

While traditional high-end Thai style was a riot of saturated colours
and intricate designs, today's approach follows the global trend of
accent rather than the complete vernacular. Subtle nuances are often
more attractive to people of other cultures and feasible for most homes.
From the simple touch of a lotus seed-pod on a coffee-table to the
extravagance of a nautilus-shell caviar spoon inlaid with scarab beetles'
wings and rubies, Siamese suggestions whisper romance and wonder.
Think of the seductive curves of a mangowood lampbase *à la* Elle
Macpherson's Bahamas beach house, the glint of gold on a glossy
black-lacquered plate, or flowers in an imposing bamboo-and-bark
basket formerly used to hold sticky rice. Now your guests are talking.

Gold Rush

One of the most elegant and exacting of Thailand's ancient crafts, gold and black lacquer painting requires at least 17 steps and 90 days to complete.

Lai rod nam ("ornaments washed with water") involves applying several coats of natural lacquer resin to wood, pottery or spun bamboo. Each layer is allowed to dry—a process which itself may take 15 to 20 days—and then polished with sandpaper and the bare human hand, the oil of which gives a wonderful sheen. A design is then painted on the piece, to which many layers of gold leaf are added (the background is covered with white latex). Each piece is then dipped in water to wash away the background, leaving behind brilliant 24k gold motifs.

In the late 18th century after Bangkok became the Thai capital, *lai rod nam* graced palace and temple pillars, window panels, screens, doors, ceremonial bowls, boxes and Buddhist scripture cabinets. Floral and vegetal patterns as well as mythical Buddhist creatures and scenes from the *Ramakian*, the Thai version of an Indian epic, were the most popular designs.

Today, contemporary designs are produced by Chiang Mai-based company Living Space. Even though it draws on traditional Thai and Japanese techniques, the lavish ornamentation is pared down to produce more spare, simpler items. Company designer Jennifer Dyson says: "My philosophy with Living Space is to develop and promote top-quality Asian crafts with a Western slant."

Above: Contemporary geometric designs on these plates by Living Space, Chiang Mai, at the Lanna Spa further the appeal of this classical craft.

Right: Gold-lacquered trinket boxes, which inspired this modern version from Living Space, were donated to temples to earn merit.

Far Right: Post-massage pampering; lemongrass tea in celadon on a gold-lacquered tray (Living Space).

Page 30: Mirror mirror on the wall. At the Lanna Spa, wooden side panels of a Burmese xylophone inlaid with mirrors, make a stunning backdrop to this over-sized sofa upholstered in Thai cotton and designed by Lek Bunnag.

Left: Doorway to heaven. Adorned with a "magical wishing tree" motif typical of Lanna *lai kham* (gold-leaf stencilling) work, a teak door in the Lanna Spa's relaxation suite blends superbly with the sybaritic surroundings. Spa and stencilling work by Lek Bunnag of Bangkok's Bunnag Architects.

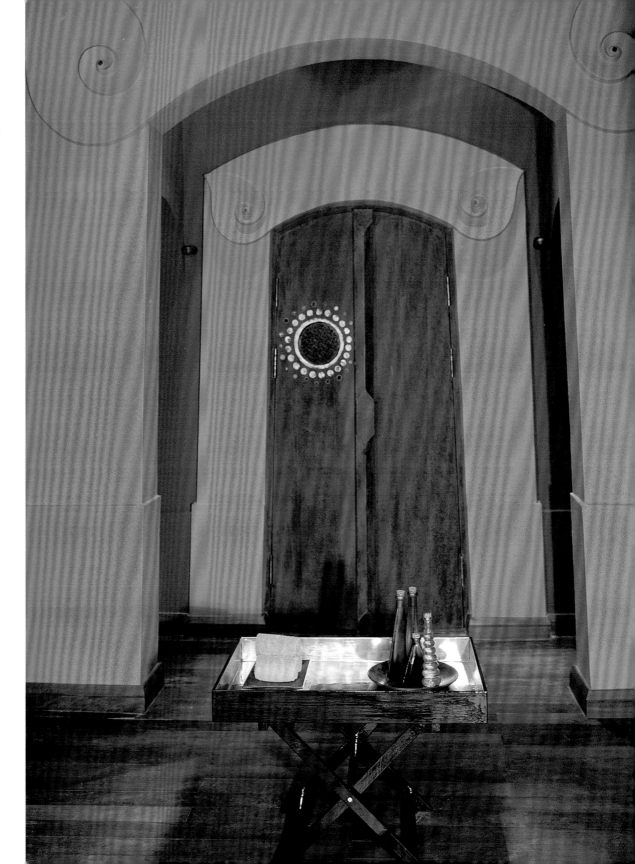

Right: The Lanna Spa massage suites await beyond a hand-hewn teak door decorated with an abstract sun motif in gold leaf. Thai aromatherapy oils such as lemongrass, ylang ylang, *prai* and nutmeg are presented on a gilded lacquer tray from Living Space, Chiang Mai.

Left: A dressing-table and mirror with *lai kham* (gold leaf) work from Gong Dee Gallery, Chiang Mai are complemented by black lacquered cosmetic boxes and bowls from Living Space, Chiang Mai, and a dramatic lamp from Earth & Fire, Bangkok.

Below: Living Space trinket boxes in red lacquer with gold geometric motifs on the lids.

Natural Resources

The high-rise Bangkok apartment of interior designer Grant Thatcher and partner Jeremy Webb is a sensual delight. Strikingly simple arrangements of dried stems, seed pods and spices serve as reminders of the earthy beginnings of his elegant furnishings. The sweet scent of cinnamon mingles with the fruity fragrance of *bael*. Philodendron foliage proffers welcome flashes of green.

Thatcher's preference for pure forms is evident in the elongated, clean lines of a pair of solid, matt, dark oak pedestal tables which he designed for the sitting room. Lacquer, "a remarkably underused finish in modern furniture despite its luxurious resonance", lends his low teak coffee-table a rich, dark brown lustre. Over-sized shallow lamp shades, again designed by Thatcher, surmount simple charcoal bases. Mango-wood bowls in intriguing forms invite further inspection. Bluish-grey walls—a refreshing alternative to white—provide a perfect foil for the dark wood in this versatile space.

Above: A terracotta pot containing cinnamon sticks and wooden bowls brimming with dried marigolds and chilli and (*right*) *bael* fruit form a creative corner composition.

Right: Lotus flowers and stems are ubiquitous emblems of Thailand.

Far Right: Dried vines and lotus-seed pods with mango-wood vases and bowls.

Left: Bold, basic furniture is softened by touches of nature such as the dried pods softly mirrored by the lacquer finish on the solid teak coffee-table. The custom-made *kachud* mat (made from the water plant *Lepironia arpiculata*) took 10 women from the southern village of Narathiwat six months to weave.

Below Left: The elegant silhouettes of mangowood containers—"the perfect artefact from a sustainable natural source," says Thatcher—complement the clean lines of a teak side table.

Below Right: In the hall, a pedestal table, designed by the owner in solid matt dark oak, serves as a stage for vials of philodendron leaves. "It's the first thing any guest sees and thus one of the most important pieces of furniture," he notes.

Honourable Intentions

With clients who include the Thai royal family, the Rajmata Gayatri Devi of Jaipur, Queen Sophia of Spain, Princess Michael of Kent and Lord David Puttnam, it is not surprising that Bangkok-based Lotus Arts de Vivre is owned and run by a family of noble descent. German aristocrat Rolf von Bueren, his Thai wife Helen and sons Sri and Nicklas—born in Thailand but schooled in England and Europe—are as culturally mixed as their *objets d'art,* jewellery and homewares.

However, it is the quality and ingenuity of its products, made from the most exotic and humble of materials, plus a commitment to preserve and revive old techniques, which sets Lotus apart.

There is a curious thrill in fingering, and possessing, fine objects made of rare materials tinged with nostalgia such as scarab beetles' wings, nautilus shell, wild boar fang and galucha (sting-ray skin). Considered holy in ancient Egypt and China where they were used to decorate temple and palace walls, the scarab beetle's wings vary from iridescent blue to green depending on the light. Lotus' craftsmen use them to adorn exquisite nautilus-shell caviar spoons and jewellery. Sting-ray leather, once the tough armour of Japanese warriors, decorates refined chairs, trays and figurines.

More mundane natural materials such as coconut shell are elevated to high art through hand-carving and the addition of precious metals and gems. Unable to be penetrated by normal wood carvers, the hard shells of

Above: A nautilus shell decorated with silver and a mother-of-pearl plate made of rare, giant oyster shell standing on sterling-silver legs and decorated with a silver elephant.

Right, from Left: Seashell ashtray with hand-wrought sterling-silver trimming; caviar spoon made from a nautilus shell decorated with facetted round rubies and scarabs' wings set in 18k gold; mother-of-pearl spoon and fork decorated with sterling silver.

Left: Yellow seashell and crystal caviar server with silver dragon stand. The eyes of the dragon, an important motif in Thai and Chinese mythology, are set with red coral.

Below Left: A mother-of-pearl spoon and fork decorated with sterling silver and a crystal caviar bowl on a mother-of-pearl tray decorated with galucha and sterling silver.

Below Right: A bamboo ashtray with hand-beaten sterling-silver trimmings and a sterling-silver beer mug with a wild boar fang handle on a wooden tray covered with mother-of-pearl.

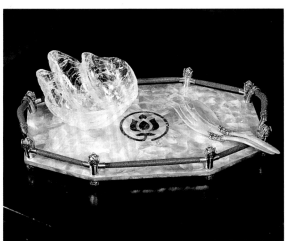

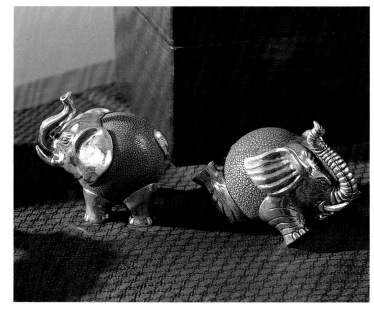

Clockwise, from Top Left: Wine bucket made from truck tyres and sterling silver. A hand-carved coconut bowl lined with sterling silver, with a sterling-silver frogs stand. Hand-carved wooden elephants, a popular design, covered with green galucha and decorated with sterling silver. Spectacle case made from carved sugar palm fruit, carved sterling-silver lined coconut goblets; and a carved coconut bowl with a sterling silver snake stand.

the coconuts and sugar-palm fruits used for tea and coffee service sets, bowls, chalices, spectacle cases, cigar holders and handbags, is worked by Asia's few remaining ivory carvers whose skills were considered obsolete after the ivory ban. Each piece takes up to three months to finish. Thai and one of India's last two damascene (gold-inlay metalwork) specialists, Nepalese gold- and silversmiths, stonecutters and setters in Rajasthan and Balinese wood-carvers are also employed. All pieces are finished in Thailand, in line with the von Bueren family's desire to retain personal design and control.

The actual design of each object is a wonderful medley of natural characteristics, Asian tradition, modern usage and sometimes, as in the case of the truck-tyre champagne bucket, pure fantasy. A porcupine toothpick holder is made of silver mounted on black onyx. A 24k-gold-leaf and lacquer-lined ostrich egg becomes a container with a Thai-style lid ornamented with rubies and set on silver stand. An electroplated conch shell is a doorstop in disguise. Even the flagship shop, in the Regent Hotel, Bangkok, is unique, with Thai-style teak floorboards pinned with wooden pegs rather than nails, low furnishings and cushions, and a policy of removing one's footwear before entering.

For those fortunate enough to afford the luxury of such individual and idiosyncratic pieces—and they include David Tang, Gianni Versace, Kenzo Takada, Roman Polanski, Gore Vidal, Elizabeth Taylor, Goldie Hawn and Shirley Bassey—Lotus is a delightful Pandora's box of style.

Above: A spathe leaf supported by a sterling-silver dragon with red-coral eyes and a coconut-shell bowl with hand-carved sterling silver on the lid are elegant accents in the Thai Suite, Peninsula Hotel, Bangkok.

Left: This hand-carved wooden frog and rooster are covered with green galucha and sterling silver.

Far Left: Sterling silver-lined coconut-shell bowl with handcrafted sterling-silver dragon handle.

Interwoven Fortunes

Basketry is another traditional Thai handicraft that is being adapted to produce modern homeware—and allow craftsmen to earn a living without sacrificing their cultural heritage. A case in point is a basket-weaving programme for Pwo Karen men from 18 villages in the remote Sop Moei District of Mae Hong Son province, west of Chiang Mai. Established by health worker Kent Gregory in 1992, the programme seeks to find functions for baskets which are all too easily being replaced by plastic buckets and polyester rice sacks.

While some tribal baskets such as the Pwo Karen's sewing baskets are reproduced exactly to size and design, others are too big to be carried aboard an aircraft or too small for modern use. The Pwos' rice-threshing basket, for instance, normally spans two metres, while their covered dome basket, used to store new blankets and clothing, dwarfs conventional clothes hampers. Both are now miniaturised to produce innovative fruit and storage or laundry containers respectively (not to mention great conversation pieces). In contrast, a palm-sized pumpkin-seed container is enlarged, given a second finely woven cover and fused with a metal stand to become an elegant wine holder.

Other innovations include bamboo and rattan serviette holders inspired by antique Thai silver betelnut-leaf holders or knife sheaths, many of which are now found on the tables of Thai embassies from Rome to Hanoi and in select boutiques in Tokyo and the French Riviera.

Opposite: Regional baskets from Sop Moei Arts in the guestroom of Lanfaa Devahastin na Ayudhaya's converted rice-barn home in Chiang Mai. A Pwo Karen clothing and blanket basket is on the floor, right. The two wicker cases are pre-war luggage pieces.

Above: Reproduction Pwo Karen sewing baskets in bamboo and rattan with teak stands. From Sop Moei Arts.

Left and Far Left: Old rattan baskets from central Thailand.

Exact replications of fine examples, particularly antiques, from other regional cultures such as garment or rice baskets from Laos, Vietnam and Burma are also made. "Our brief to our weavers is to copy the original in such faithful detail that, if sent to the people from which the models originate, they would swear that it was one of their own," says Gregory. Apart from *objets d'art* in their own right, these baskets make distinctive vases, fruit or pot-pourri containers and trinket boxes.

Two other indigenous Thai styles of basketry, under the patronage of Queen Sirikit's Support Foundation, are experiencing a resurgence as home-decor accents. A northeast handicraft, *khit* bamboo basketry was once so threatened that only one family in Kalasin province was able to pass on the necessary skills to the foundation. The complicated process involves finding suitable bamboo *(phai rai)*, leaving it to dry, splitting it into tiny strips and dyeing some of them to make woven patterns. Other parts of the bamboo are cut into bigger pieces to form a frame. The dyed and undyed tiny strips are then interwoven within the structure to form a desired pattern. Rattan is used for the rim and handle.

A southern Thai tradition, *yan lipao* basket-weaving is named after the strong and durable vine used throughout the Ratanakosin Period to make household items such as trays, betel baskets and betel bowls. Many of these were decorated with gold, silver, copper and ivory. Taking up to six months per basket to make, *yan lipao* basketry was a languishing craft until Queen Sirikit had her handbags made from it for her overseas tours and used *yan lipao* serving containers for her banquets.

Left: Basket cases. *Khit* bamboo baskets from Tamnan Mingmuang, Bangkok. Those in foreground are used to hold sticky rice in Khalasin province, while the one in the background is a *Khit* bamboo vase, an adapted version woven over a terracotta vase.

Opposite, Far Left: An old bamboo and rattan fruit basket from central Thailand.

Above: A favourite of Queen Sirikit of Thailand, these tightly woven *yan lipao* baskets are woven by Muslim craftsmen in Narathiwat province, southern Thailand.

Top: With their lids carved to resemble mangosteens and pumpkins, these bowls woven from *sam liam* grass by the Htin hill tribe in Nan province, northern Thailand are ideal for serving or storing condiments. From Tamnan Mingmuang.

Right: Bamboo and rattan serviette holders, with a fine black banding taken from a detail in an antique Lao basket, are shaped like traditional Thai silver betel-nut leaf holders. The shape of the rattan wine holder comes from a basket that was originally used to store pumpkin seeds. From Sop Moei Arts.

Below: A Laotian rice-storage basket fitted at the top with an antique Burmese gong is a unique lamp base from Sop Moei Arts, Chiang Mai.

Dramatic
Table Settings

Kenzo to Donna Karan, Polanski to David Putnam; countless *farangs* (foreigners) have been inspired by the Thais' entertaining élan. Their innate sense of hospitality or *nam sai jai jing* ("water from the heart") begins in the villages, where terracotta water jars are placed at the entrance of each home for thirsty guests and strangers alike. At the other extreme, no expense is spared during the annual Loi Krathong (lunar new year) festival, for which countless manhours go into making candlelit floral floats *(krathong)* and pandanus-leaf baskets containing mouthwatering morsels. From minimalist to retro-fusion, the possibilities for decorating your table Thai-style are endless.

Previous Page: A Western-style table setting at the author's Chiang Mai home, Sri Deva Giri ("God's prosperous hill"). Sukhothai-style plates and bowls are from Kingdom of Father Ceramic, Bangkok. Contemporary cups from Earth & Fire, Bangkok. Home-dried leaves and flowers form the napkin rings and centrepiece. Cutlery with burl wood handles from Nawaporn, Bangkok.

Right: Courtyard chic. This contemporary setting at Vila Cini, Chiang Mai, is casually elegant. The silk tablecloth and runner are from Vila Cini; flatware is yellow celadon from Oriental Style, Chiang Mai.

Alfresco

Open-air dining is an integral part of Thailand's tropical lifestyle. The upper classes would traditionally eat in a separate dining pavilion or *sala*. Because they had no walls (like the Balinese *balé*), they encouraged the free flow of air. Often raised, these roofed platforms were (and are today) often built near rivers or lakes to enhance ventilation and provide relief from the heat and humidity. Villagers would sit on the stoop of their houses or underneath them for their meals. The *suan ahaan* (garden restaurant) is today universally popular throughout the country. In the same way, even in metropolitan plots, people build a *sala*—to eat in, to relax in, or simply to take in the evening air and the scents from a floral garden.

Modern translations of this alfresco tradition are the sit-down *soirée* under the stars and the picnic buffet, ideally riverside or in a beautiful garden.

Up-to-the-minute items such as yellow celadon, durable, double-woven, silk napkins and place-mats, and hand-beaten stainless-steel cutlery embody a new no-fuss approach to entertaining. Simple candles surrounded by fresh chrysanthemums or a spray of orchids make a charmingly informal and easily arranged centrepiece.

While your guests are tucking into their Thai beef salad *(yam nue)*, you can casually mention that the unusual shade of their celadon was achieved by varying the amount of oxygen in a kiln outside Chiang

Top and Above: Cutting-edge. Thai warriors traditionally valued above all else a sword made in Aranyik, near Ayuthaya. Continuing this craftsmanship is N.V. Aranyik Company Limited, which produces high-quality tableware for both domestic use and for export.

Left: Place-mats woven from double-silk threads from Vila Cini, Chiang Mai, have modern patterns.

This Page and Opposite:
Red, black and blue. The Ping River's cool tones are an ideal counterpoint to this contemporary range of flatware from Earth & Fire, Bangkok. The simple straw place-mats and napkin holders are from Nawaporn, Bangkok, while the "snail-handle" cutlery is from N.V. Aranyik Company Limited, Ayuthaya. Photographed at Chiang Mai's Baan Suan restaurant.

Mai; or drop into the conversation that the cutlery originates from a small village near Ayuthaya once famous for producing the best swords. From cunning craft to conversation piece, Thai tableware enhances the elegant outdoor dining experience.

One of the advantages of buffets or smorgasbords is that guest numbers can be flexible and the atmosphere generally more relaxed and informal than a sit-down affair, as diners are freer to mingle and move about.

In keeping with the unpretentious atmosphere, the flatware should be durable, simple and strong both in appearance and performance. These requirements are fulfilled by most modern Thai ceramics.

Bangkok-based Earth & Fire, for example, makes contemporary ceramics that mimic the country-style earthenware of the past. The strong, earthy colours and bold designs complement other rustic elements such as straw place-mats and napkin holders adapted from traditional fishing-knife sheaths woven from bamboo. Casually assembled cutlery, stacks of plates and light tasty dishes such as stir-fried noodles *(phad Thai)* are an inviting combination.

The addition of a fabulous fruit basket (think exotic varieties such as mangosteens, mangoes, starfruit and rambutans, but avoid the evil-smelling durian), garden-picked greenery (banana and philodendron leaves make great place-mats or table runners) and ethnic accessories such as lunar new year lanterns can transport your table to Thailand without too much effort. After all, most Thais believe that the best activities in life should be *sanuk* (fun).

Opposite: At Baan Suan restaurant, banana-leaf cones cleverly cover water glasses. The flatware, from Mae Rim Ceramics in Chiang Mai, shows Japanese as well as Lanna influences.

Left: A table from Gerard Collection complements the green lattice design of woven bamboo flatware from Earth & Fire, Bangkok.

Below: Light relief. Traditional cotton-cloth lanterns are suspended from trees on the restaurant's riverside terrace. At lunar new year in northern Thailand, these lanterns are hung outside houses and temples.

Fun Fusion

It's pairing Western-style place-mats with organically shaped noodle bowls or serving caviar in a coconut shell. It's drawing on natural and traditional materials to inspire texture, colour and form, from the crimson of a hill-tribe turban to the sheerness of shantung; the ash-grey of incense on an altar to the age-grain of wood. It's using inheritance as a reference and imagination as a referee. It's fun, it's funky, it's fusion.

The Thais have always been open to other influences, as long as they complement their own culture, and nowhere is this more celebrated than on the table. From the commissioning of Chinese celadon and Indian brocade with Thai motifs as far back as the 14th century, to the current poaching of craft techniques and styles from Bali, Myanmar and Japan, the Thais are masters at distilling the best from eclectic sources.

Home-grown companies such as Cocoon are tapping into global trends for fresh takes on Thai-and-true methods and materials. Ceramics, glass, textiles, furnishings, candles, cutlery and ephemeral crafts such as floristry and fruit carving are all experiencing a revival as entertaining in the home and in restaurants competes with television as the number-one mode of relaxing.

Fusion style, like fusion food, means respecting the past without repeating it. It marries modern tastes with ancient emphases on quality and individuality. At tonight's dinner party, carefully crafted items with a twist are *de rigueur;* mass-produced objects have become as unpalatable as mass-produced food.

Right: Trend-setting. This contemporary Asian table setting from Bangkok-based Cocoon is completely global in feel—and completely produced in Thailand. Imported Japanese techniques and colours are used to achieve the crackled glazing on the ceramics. The holes in the noodle bowls offer an alternative place to rest the hand-carved rosewood chopsticks other than on the Thai silk place-mats. The chairs are teak woven with leather.

Below: Reflected glory. Two-tone hand-finished cutlery from Cocoon, Bangkok, looks good enough to eat with.

Bottom: Naturally gifted. Organic shapes grant each piece a surprising and uncompromising individuality.

Traditional—with a Twist

"Jim Thompson was the most famous host of his time; he served quite awful food but no-one ever remembers it that way because the settings of his house were so spectacular."
—Author and long-term Bangkok resident, William Warren

Thompson, the famous American credited with reviving Thailand's silk industry in the 1950s and '60s, was the first internationally known expatriate to make an art form of Thai-style decorating when entertaining. He was certainly not the last.

Fashion designer Kenzo is well-known for the exotic parties held at his seaside villa at the Amanpuri, Phuket. A guest at one of his Thai buffets remembers fabulously carved fruits *(salak)* in the shapes of mythical birds and beasts. Actress Geena Davis and her film director husband Renny Harlin floated *krathongs* comprising candles, incense sticks and flowers in the swimming-pool of their private pavilion for their wedding reception at the Banyan Tree Phuket. Somerset Maugham, Noel Coward, Barbara Cartland and James Mitchener were all delighted with the receptions they received at the Oriental Hotel; Gore Vidal continues to spend his winters at The Oriental in Bangkok, as does Frederick Forsythe and Elaine Paige at Banyan Tree Phuket, both establishments renowned for their impeccable food and service.

Left and Above: Naga House in Bangkok lends a charming feel to the setting. Traditionally a mark of royalty, the elephant has long been revered in Thai society, and is an obvious motif for these contemporary crystal glasses.

Bencharong tea and dinner sets, crystal glasses and bronze cutlery are all from Naga House, Bangkok.

Right: Bencharong and *bai-sri* in celebrationary green, red and gold are complemented by old *phasins* (tubular skirts) from Maya, Bangkok. Each *bai-sri* is made from banana leaves decorated with a pink lotus blossom topped with a finial of crown flowers and crepe jasmines. Petal-folded lotus blossoms, gardenias and dendrobium orchids nestle at its base. Delicate jasmine strings encircle the Thai silk napkins. Styling by Sakul Intakul studio.

Below: Covered casserole dishes such as this one, and even the idea of individual place settings, are distinctly foreign concepts.

Below Right: Bencharong tea sets also reflect Western influence. The *lai nam thong* motif, however dates back to the time of Rama II.

Below and Opposite: Old red-lacquered *khantokes* support bowls—their insides glazed with celadon, their outsides unglazed—from Mae Rim Ceramics, Chiang Mai. The cotton napkins are from Paya, Bangkok. Spicy pork sausage *(sai oua)* and pickled pork sausage *(naem)* are typical *khantoke* fare.

Right: A jasmine *malai* (garland), which here adds a finishing touch to these *khantoke* sets, is a traditional Lanna offering to welcome guests. The more elaborate and intricate garlands are offered to royalty, dignatories and foreign guests.

Ever since Louis XIV of France ate from gold and silver cutlery given to him by King Narai the Great of Ayuthaya (1658–88), classical Thai tableware and ornaments have enhanced dining in other cultures. Bencharong, celadon, brown and blue-and-white ceramic flatware, complemented by lacquerware, silver and gold accessories, can all be used for romantic and highly dramatic effects.

Classical northern Thai *khantokes* (large trays with foot bases) are another versatile and fun dining option. Each *khantoke* traditionally held enough food for an individual diner; usually one dry curry, one chilli paste, one pickled sausage dish, a vegetable dish and almost always crispy pork skin *(kab moo)*. Intricately woven baskets containing sticky rice would rest on the *khantoke* or the mat on which the diners sat (with or without cushions). As cutlery or chopsticks were not used, bowls of water for handwashing were also provided.

Above: Silver lacquerware (cup, coaster and napkin ring) from Living Space, Chiang Mai, and a sprig of golden shower *(Cassia fistula),* Thailand's national flower, complement this contemporary blue-and- white china from Paya, Bangkok. The antique Thai table in teak with rattan inset is from Naga House, Bangkok. Chopsticks and cutlery from N. V. Aranyik Company Limited complete this attractive ensemble.

Since its origins in China more than 1,000 years ago (and its huge output by the Japanese) blue-and-white china has been beloved around the world. In Thailand, the crisp colour combination knows a myriad forms—turquoise Siamese-cat eyes rimmed with creamy fur; the irridescent indigo and ivory of silk; an azure sky peppered with pearly clouds. It is little wonder the Thais are so fond of it for their dining tables. Both locally made and imported versions have been used since the 14th century; many of those from China show distinctly Chinese motifs such as peony flowers, which are not native to Thailand.

Perfect for occasions requiring a little extra class, contemporary or antique blue-and-white china is both pretty and practical. It can be dressed up with silver, lacquerware and fresh flowers and works well with most ethnic fabrics, from intricately patterned *batik* and *ikat* to textured silk and linen.

Contemporary blue-and-white is, in fact, so endemic in Asia that popular designs are easily replaceable and mandatory in most kitchen cupboards. Another advantage is that the different designs and shades of blue-and-white—from cobalt to the palest sky tones—complement each other so effectively that a complete set of one pattern is hardly necessary. In fact, mixing and matching within this genre is fun and encourages collecting from a wide range of sources.

Above: These indigo *ikat mon kwang* cushions from Paya are traditionally placed at the user's right-hand side for resting between courses.

Left and Far Left: Blue-and-white ware from Paya. The unglazed blue-and-white bowl features Wat Phumin, one of the most beautiful and distinctive Lanna temples in Nan province, northern Thailand. All of Paya's blue-and-white pieces reproduce traditional Thai motifs.

An exotic mood can be also achieved through the ephemeral art of *salak* (fruit and vegetable carving). This entails such a level of skill that ever since the Ayuthaya era, when it originated in the women's quarter of the royal court, it has been classified as a *chang* (craft) in its own right. Rolf von Bueren, patriach of luxury boutique chain Lotus Arts de Vivre, discovered the wonder of *salak* when he dined at the house of a Thai prince: "The whole dinner from beginning to end was carved. Five minutes later it was all destroyed. The fact you could digest such craftsmanship impressed me tremendously."

While some of the more intricate designs should be left to the experts, simpler ways of carving food items such as pineapples and pumpkins can be easily achieved by the layman. Carved pumpkins traditionally contain a Thai dessert made from egg and coconut milk, *sankaya*, but are equally attractive receptacles for Western soups and Eastern curries and wet dishes. Hollowed-out pineapples, cut horizontally or vertically, are great not only for fruit salad but for fried rice and curry dishes. Large fruits such as melon and papaya, cut in the shape of boats or birds, are ideal for holding simple desserts such as cantaloupe and watermelon balls or side dishes of cucumber and carrot.

Right: Carved pumpkins hold a spicy vegetable soup called *gaeng liang* but can also be used for Western soups such as pumpkin and vichyssoise. Monstera leaves are lush place-mats, while the napkin holders are folded from Flame of the Forest leaves decorated with Champaka flowers. Candles and Frangipani flowers are placed on Ching Dynasty five-colour ware, from which Thai bencharong originated. The cutlery is from N.V. Aranyik Company Limited.

Far Right Top: Beef curry *(gaeng ped nuea)* and fried rice *(khao phat)* are served in pineapples.

Far Right Bottom: Watermelon and papaya "boats" make innovative receptacles.

Another craft, known as *bai-sri*, the art of making exquisite folded banana-leaf and floral arrangements for religious offerings, adds a romantic, retro-fusion feel. Filled with cooked rice and often topped with boiled eggs, a version called *bai-sri pak cham* is used to consecrate spirit houses or in other ceremonies of Brahman origin. More simple *bai-sri* were traditionally given to children when they reached four days old, at the cutting of the top-knot ceremony and during monk's ordination ceremonies.

Other floral arrangements called *phoum*, usually about 20cm high with their base in a bowl, resemble colourful pieces of porcelain. These are made with the purple or white *Gomphrena globosa* or Bachelor's Button flower which is dried and dyed, then arranged in an intricate spiral. Because they are dried arrangements and thus long-lasting, they are often placed in front of pictures of the king and in cemeteries. Even *malai* (garlands) make picturesque table decorations or napkin rings.

Serve *tom yam goong* (hot and sour prawn soup) with a Western main course or *som tam* (papaya salad) followed by an Indian curry, each in its appropriate flatware, add Thai accents such as *mat mee* (Thai *ikat*) table linen, and your guests could be excused for thinking they have stumbled into Jim Thompson's dining room—minus the awful food, of course!

Above: Salty eggs gleam like jewels on a coronet of banana leaves which festively mark each setting.

Right: Highly strung. An intricate garland *(malai)* of jasmine, crown flowers and rose petals lies coiled in a blue-and-white stem vase.

Far Right: Enchanted forest. Black-coral "trees" appear to blossom with jasmine in these typically Oriental arrangements.

Above: Guests at Nagara Sambandaraksa's table must literally turn over a new leaf (or two) before they are at liberty to dine. An antique Japanese silk *obi* or kimono sash is used as a table runner.

Thai Fabrics
Old and New

The costumes of 17th-century Thai delegates caused such a sensation in France that the word 'Siamoise' was soon synonymous with silk. Thanks to supporters such as Jim Thompson and Queen Sirikit, the world continues to be seduced by Thai silk which graces the homes of Leonardo di Caprio, Tony Blair and Hillary Clinton. But not all of Thailand's fabulous fabrics are cut from the same cloth. Hand-woven natural fibres like cotton, hemp, pineapple and banana glow with dyes made from vegetables, bark, soil and even cow dung. From cushions to curtains, sofas to serviettes, the future looms bright for Thai textiles.

Moral Fibre

Cushioning the blow to Thailand's traditional textile-weaving societies are a variety of local companies catering to the global home-decor market. Threatened by the exodus of young people from villages to the cities and the influx of cheap alternative products to once-thriving rural areas, the future of crafts such as textile weaving was, literally, hanging by a thread a decade ago.

Says Kent Gregory of Sop Moei Arts, Chiang Mai: "All over Thailand textile weaving is vastly underpaid and all too often only older people are doing it. To make learning these skills attractive to young people, we have to offer incentives so that they can earn not a subsistence living, but one that offers hope for themselves and their children. This means paying three to five times more than similar activities earn in the rest of this country. It means too that we have to work hard to produce unique items the markets will bear."

As the contemporary applications of handwoven cotton, silk, hemp and linen on these and following pages reveal, Bangkok-based companies such as Cocoon, Jim Thompson and Khomapastr, and their Chiang Mai counterparts including K Textiles, Fai Ngam, Sop Moei Arts and Living Space, are doing just that. By reviving the demand for dying traditions and also producing items that are both fashionable and of a high quality, they are bringing new dignity to talented artisans and their families.

Above: Cotton on to the beauty of natural fibre, here pleated for extra textural interest. From Cocoon.

Right: Ribbons of hemp from the Golden Triangle are woven into these unusual Cocoon cushions.

Previous Page: At the Sukhothai Hotel, Bangkok, Jim Thompson Thai silk bestows an opalescent sheen to furnishings by Chantaka Puranananda for Pure Design, Bangkok.

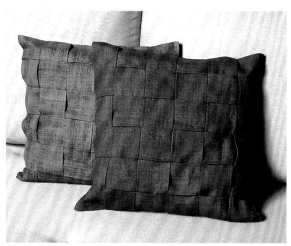

Above: Different textures add definition to simply shaped teak furniture from Cocoon. Natural-colour Thai linen covers the sofa cushions while its frame is upholstered in dark blue velvet.

Far Left: Squares of Thai and Burmese *ikat* silks called *mat mee* are juxtaposed in these Cocoon cushions.

Left: Thai silk and Chinese *cheongsam* toggles lend a subtle sophistication to any sofa. From Cocoon.

Homage to Hemp

Once relegated in the West to making sacks and other utilitarian items, hemp is now holding its own as a beautiful and versatile fabric source for the home. Interior designers and their suppliers are inspired by the Hmong, Karen and Lahu minority tribes in Thailand who for centuries have depended on the durable fibre for homespun items as diverse as aprons, turbans, sashes, money bags, burial clothes and rugs.

The cloth is woven from the *katom* plant, the leaf of which looks similar to marijuana but is not the same. Some of the mainly women weavers still use a body tension loom with a back strap and foot treadle, meaning that only narrow widths, no wider than the slim waists to which they are anchored, can be produced.

Drawing on ancient natural dyeing techniques, producers such as K Textiles directed by Kachamas Kirathipumtam are using vegetal, mineral and organic matter to create a rainbow of exotic shades: blue from the indigo plant and pineapple leaves; tangerine, mauve and shocking pink from seeds and roots; lilac and brown from vegetables and fruits; green and grey from ashes; brown and magenta from soil and cow dung.

Minute needles are used for intricate embroidery. Apart from traditional animal and plant motifs, each family has its own symbolic design which leads to more variations than the tartans of Scotland and Ireland. With modern applications of hand-woven hemp, a baby's jacket could well inspire an elegant bedspread.

Left: Hardly humble. This hemp bedspread in Chairat Kamonorathep's Chiang Mai home is hand-embroidered with hundreds of tiny natural pearls. Bedspread, table runner and cushions from K Textiles, Chiang Mai.

Far Left: Cushions such as these from K Textiles use completely natural fibres (in this case, hemp, but cotton, silk, pineapple and banana fibres are also woven by the company) and dyes. Their production supports the continuation of traditional crafts by Thailand's hill tribe people.

Opposite and This Page:
Bags of style. Handwoven cotton from K Textiles photographed at the verandah of Chairat Kamonorathep's typical old Lanna House. Such bolts of cloth have an array of modern uses—from casual throws on the back of a sofa to place-mats and cushions.

Spinning Yarns

The story of how the home-spun homewares on these pages were conceived is a rollicking good one. In 1977, Thailand-born Kent Gregory started public health work in a Pwo Karen tribal enclave about 300km west of Chiang Mai. The area was so remote that these people lived much as they had for centuries. While extremely poor, their tradition of arts and crafts—such as weaving and basketry—flourished out of necessity and their small rice-farming villages had struck a balance with nature.

Then, in 1988, this status quo began to unravel as roads were built. Merchants began to drive to the area, selling cheap ready-made clothing and plastic containers. To gain money for these purchases, the villagers were persuaded to plant vast areas of chillies which the merchants would then buy. Correspondingly large tracts of virgin forest were cleared and streams damaged. There was no longer a need to keep the old skills alive.

Determined to stop this destruction of cultural and natural resources, Gregory introduced in 1993 a textile-weaving programme for the women, a basket-weaving program (see page 43) for the men and coffee-planting as an alternative to slash-and-burn agriculture.

In consultation with international design consultants, over a six-year period, Gregory selected and simplified designs which could be traced back to local ethnic (Karen) or regional (Thai, Lao or Burmese) textiles.

Opposite: Inspired by Songkran (lunar new year) wall hangings, these three dramatic pieces of art, titled *Sukhothai, Lanna* and the award-winning *Indigo Dawn,* use different yarns but the same motif found on a sarong from Nan province. They are from Sop Moei Arts, Chiang Mai, photographed in Serm Phenjati's house.

Left: A modern version of a low Oriental seating arrangement, this Sop Moei Arts puzzle sofa features expandable modules of "male" and "female" pieces with reversible tie-on cushions in cotton-silk with gold thread. The complementary Japanese-style floor cushions are in cotton and gold.

Above: The weaving process for this spectacular gold, yellow and blue table runner is tediously slow. Three different shuttles with three different yarns are used for each line woven, superimposing one pattern upon another, giving it a suble shifting of colour. From Sop Moei Arts.

"Asian textiles are often such a rich riot of colour and motif that, unless they are collected just to look at, they are difficult to sell outside of this country," says Gregory. "My job is to give a new textile just that ethnic touch so that it can be placed in contemporary settings, adding elegance and intrigue rather than staring its owner out of the house."

Typically the consultants spent six weeks working with Gregory and the hill-tribe weavers to create new textiles for soft interior furnishings or fashion. A year later, they would return to the villages to find their original patterns reproduced in a variety of exciting and experimental ways to form a whole collection. Sop Moei Arts was born.

"As Thailand reaches out to include the hill tribes, much of the rich diversity found in these tribal areas is being lost," Gregory notes. "The feeling back in the mountains is that Thai is better. What I am fighting for is the awareness that Pwo Karen arts, crafts and ways are just as valid."

Thus, for example, a Pwo woman's blouse inspires a palette of reds, pinks and yellows, supplemented by the indigo of the trousers of field-workers, to create an international award-winning wall hanging called *Indigo Dawn*.

Hopefully, with companies such as Sop Moei Arts, the sun will never set on these once dying arts.

Above: Surprisingly contemporary, the block pattern on this silk bedspread from Sop Moei Arts comes from a hill-tribe in southern Laos.

Right and Far Right: The embroidery patterns used for these Living Space cushions made of hemp cloth by the Hmong tribes are at least 20 years old. Their soft, muted colours recall the days when the dyes used were completely natural.

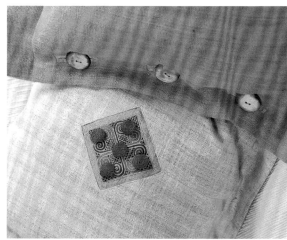

Rustic Chic

We may not all live in a converted rice-barn nestled in the foothills around Chiang Mai, but that does not mean we cannot enjoy a rustic respite. The warmth and comfort of homespun cotton, not to mention the vivid tones produced by natural indigo dye, are revelations.

So too are the thought processes that lie behind the designs. A blue-tufted bedspread from Sop Moei Arts, for instance, draws on three hill-tribe fabrics for its inspiration. The designs come from a Karen man's shoulder bag and a married woman's blouse, while the tufts or pom-poms are like those found on the dresses of unmarried girls. The bright cross-stitches on the centre patchwork of cushions from the same company trace the patterns sewn with seeds in traditional garments.

Fabrics by the bolt, small floor rugs and runners, cushion and pillow covers and table linen produced by Chaing Mai locals are among Fai Ngam's best-selling items. "Cotton is the king of fabrics, strong and cool while silk is the queen of fabrics, lush and elegant," says Bung-Earn Wongwigayakam of Fai Ngam. The electric blues and vibrant hues of these hand-woven fabrics look especially good against wood or bamboo. Use these exquisite ethnic pieces to dress up the canopy of a bed or a veranda rail and feel the lure of "the land of a million rice fields" as the Lanna Kingdom was called.

Above and Right: Homespun cotton fabrics with natural indigo dye from Fai Ngam, Chiang Mai, photographed in Lanfaa Devahastin na Ayudhaya's converted rice barn.

Opposite: Variations on a dream. Along with the blue-tufted bedspread, the centre patchwork on the naturally dyed indigo cotton cushions are taken from married hill-tribe women's blouses. Bedspread and baskets from Sop Moei Arts, Chiang Mai.

Pièce de Résistance

When a famous Italian fashion designer recently ordered 100m of *mat mee* silk with gold thread from Thailand for the walls of his summer villa's dining room, a 15-month wait was not quite what he had in mind. As Jennifer Dyson of Chiang Mai-based Living Space recalls, "The result was incredibly beautiful but nerve-wracking, to say the least, as this craft cannot be rushed. The deadlines were coming from New York where life beats at a rather different pace."

Mat mee, the Thai term for the more internationally known Indonesian word *ikat,* is an intricate resist-dye technique in which the yarns for the weft are tied with water-proof strings to resist the dye and thus create a pattern in the weft yarns before they are woven. This sophisticated version of the once popular tie-and-dye method was originally used to create the *phanung* skirt-cloths of women and the *chong kaben* pantaloons of men. A 3.6-metre panel would take four months' preparation and weaving time; little wonder that a 100-metre masterpiece in the finest four-ply silk took almost four times as long to make.

One of the reasons for the slow production time is that there are no written instructions so only a few talented artisans have acquired this skill verbally over generations stretching back 800 years. Much of the original influence came from India, from where Thai royalty and aristocrats commissioned *patola* silk panels before this skill was acquired in northeast Thailand.

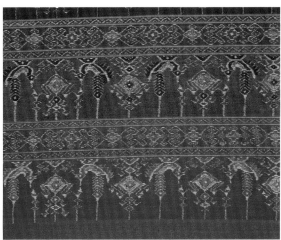

Far Left: A selection of textile holders *(mai khan)* carved to resemble *naga* and *kanok* (flaming leaves).

Left: Several traditional patterns, of Khmer origin, are combined in these *mat mee* panels from Living Space, Chiang Mai. To the left, a wooden finial from a Thai temple called a *chofa* surveys the scene like a graceful bird. On the right the base of a red-and-gold lacquered Lanna manuscript cabinet supports a Lanna-style gold-lacquered offering tray.

Above: Details of *mat mee* panels from Living Space.

Thread of Life

From the cottages of women weavers in northeast Thailand to the homes of the likes of US Secretary of State Madeline Albright and actor Leonardo De Caprio, Thai silk undergoes a complex production process using the most ancient and the most modern of techniques.

Captive *Bombyx mori* moths lay thousands of eggs which hatch into worms. After spending one month munching mulberry leaves and increasing their body weight by 10,000 times, they spin golden silk cocoons. These are then blasted with hot air to kill the moths before they eat their way out of the cocoons. An unbroken thread is then spun by machine from several size-sorted cocoons at one time. The spun silk is then bleached and dyed before it is woven by local village women in their homes.

According to legend, silk originated in China more than 4,000 years ago when a concubine accidentally dropped a cocoon into hot water and found that it unravelled into a tensile thread. China remained the main source of the world's silks until the 1920s, when Japan took over.

It was not until the 1940s, when American architect Jim Thompson arrived in Bangkok on military service, that anyone had seriously contemplated the possibility of creating a global market for Thai silk. Although intrinsic to many parts of Thailand's rural cultures, it was no match even for the industries of France and

Above: Chequered history. Inspired by the patterns on upcountry men's sarongs, the "Sumter" design on these Queen Ann chairs is a classic at Jim Thompson.

Right: Always a favourite, the cream sofa in durable cotton is at home in most living rooms. This turn-leg sofa in "Savoy" Thai cotton designed by Prinya for Jim Thompson is no exception.

Above: A bench upholstered in "Wentworth" silk-cotton-polyester mix reflects the boutique's eclectic range of home furnishings.

Italy. However, with the disruption to the predominant silk producers caused by World War II, Thompson saw a window of opportunity. He persuaded some weavers who were working as plumbers to make some samples and went abroad.

By 1952, after Thompson's silk featured in *Harper's Bazaar* and *Vogue*, along with the costumes of the stage version of *The King and I,* the value of Thai silk exports had quadrupled over just two years. By 1959 it was 11 million baht—20 times the 1950 figure. Queen Sirikit had Pierre Balmain design her wardrobe in it, and her Support Foundation continues to promote Thai silk both locally and overseas. Now Jim Thompson makes enough fabric yearly to run from one end of the country to the other.

Ever since it was smuggled in a walking cane to Europe from the court of Constantinople, the "queen of cloth" has been associated with romance and mystery. The sudden disappearance of the father of Thai silk in 1967 in Malaysia continues this tradition. One thing is certain: Thailand's largest export has come a long way from the days when Thompson was selling samples from his arm in the lobby of Bangkok's Oriental Hotel.

Opposite: Turn-leg sofa in "Savoy" cotton by Prinya for Jim Thompson.

Clockwise from Opposite Bottom Right: A war elephant, an Oriental pagoda, a jungle tiger on an elephant's back with a leopard motif background, an elephant in a parade and a war elephant with palm trees are among the exotic designs on a recent range of cushions by Jim Thompson.

By Royal Decree

Once exclusively reserved for royal attire, *pha geow phim tong* ("gold printed fabric"), like many traditional Thai crafts, was in danger of extinction by World War II. Enchanted by the costumes of their ancestors, Prince Bovaradej and Princess Pachongrajitr Kritabara of Hua Hin established Khomapastr in 1948 to dye and print colour and gold patterns. The name of the company is derived from the word *khoma* (white) and *pastr* (fabric) as the base for the work was always white fabric. The company is still the only one in Thailand to produce this exquisite material which can be seen at Vimanmek Palace (the old residence of King Chulalongkorn) and the National Theatre in Bangkok.

For centuries *pha yang* (as the process was originally known—the Thai word for "simple fabric") was hand-painted by artists using tree sap. The pattern was subsequently filled in using natural dyes and, where appropriate, gold leaf. In ancient times, the latter part of the process was done in India; eventually everything was executed in Thailand. Nowadays, wood-block printing rather than hand-painting creates the intricate patterns and the factory is in Bangkok, but the rest of the production techniques remain the same.

So does the fabric's patrons which include presidents and the royal family—although they are more likely to use it on pillows, tables, curtains, chairs and sofas than on their backs.

Right: Illustrious company. Enjoyed by royalty and heads of state, Khomapastr's *pha geow phim tong* fabric was used to upholster furniture supplied by Jim Thompson in the rarefied Thai suite of the Peninsula Hotel, Bangkok.

Far Right, Top, Centre and Bottom: Gold-leaf block painting originally executed in India to Thai specifications, transforms these Khomapastr cushions into works of art.

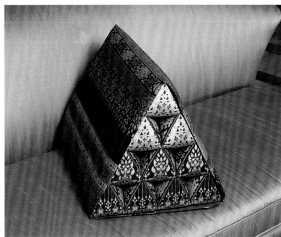

Traditional Textiles

Framed or displayed on a textile holder, traditional Thai textiles make fabulous features in the home. They can also be used as table runners or draped over statuary or chairs for an eye-catching ethnic touch.

The Thais have long used textiles as decor to convey prestige and elegance as well as serve practical functions. In the late Ayuthaya and Bangkok eras, *pha kiao* (pillar cloths) served as wall hangings, curtains, room partitions, throne and seating-platform covers, ceremonial cloths, floor coverings and carpets. They were also the main decoration for Buddhist temples, demarcating sacred and secular spaces, as well as wrappers to protect delicate palm-leaf Buddhist scriptures.

Locally made and imported textiles were also worn by the Thai monarchy and nobility to denote rank. As far back as the 17th century, Thai women favoured black for attire, often brocaded with gold and silver. Motifs included vegetation such as sandal and lotus flowers and flaming leaves *(kanok)*, and mythical figures, angels, nymphs, Garuda (a mythical bird), *nagas* (semi-divine snakes) and lions *(rajasingh* or *norasingh)*. Indigenous patterns included *chok, tiin jok, khit, mat mee* and *muk.*

Because of their quality and beauty, textiles have long been used by Thailand as commodities to forge diplomatic and commercial relationships with foreigners. Today's growing demand for these items for interior decoration continues this exciting dialogue.

Left: Traditional *mat mee* with gold thread from Isaan in northeast Thailand.

Right: Warp factor. The upper left textile is an example of the rare *muk* supplementary warp technique still used today in the *phasins* (skirts) of the Tai Phuan and Tai Yuan tribes (of Laotion origin) in the Sukhothai and Utteradit provinces. Old *chok* textiles from the same areas are also displayed.

Below: Exquisite examples of Chok design from the Sukhothai province.

Bottom: A Lanna banner or *tung,* of loosely woven cotton, made as an offering to the Buddha.

New Trends
in Bamboo & Rattan

From intricate Japanese tea-sets to Indonesian *angklung* orchestras, spidery scaffolding on Hong Kong high-rises to melodic Malaysian wind-chimes, bamboo has always been an emblem of the East. Thailand's commonest craft material is rooting out slower growing, heavier competitors to take its place at the head (and base) of dining tables of distinction, not to mention sofa suites, shelves, coffee-tables and beds. Rattan and other pliable plants are likewise creeping up the style stakes as elegant alternatives for home furnishings. No longer lightweights in the interiors arena, these sustainable shoots are the subject of international conventions and intimate conversations. Even the conservatives are trying this good grass.

Pliable Personality

Considering that typical Thai village houses do not contain much, if any, furniture, the very concept of Thai-made chairs, dining-tables, sofas and beds is a response to foreign fashions. Indeed, the main clients of quality furniture shops such as Pataya Furniture Collection, Bangkok, are foreigners living in or visiting Thailand. Australian model Elle Macpherson recently revealed a fondness for richly textured rattan when she unveiled her colonial-style beach house in the Bahamas.

While the designs are definitely driven by global trends, the materials—in Pataya's case, rattan—are undoubtedly local, as is the painstaking production process. Used in rural crafts such as basketry, the supple stems of the climbing *Calamus* palm give home accessories and furniture a natural finish which can be as sleek and fine as fabric. Wicker—plaited twigs or willow—is also used.

The newest direction for rattan and the even more ubiquitous bamboo is that it is creeping from the garden terrace and veranda into the bedroom, living room and dining room—not just in eco-friendly resorts and beach houses, but in townhouses, high-rise apartments and other metropolitan settings. As with other ethnic elements, the emphasis is on accent rather than overkill. Whether rattan adds texture to an otherwise starkly simple table-top or lamp shade or complements the dark wood frames of high-backed dining chairs, a little goes a long way towards contemporary Thai style.

Right: Upholstered with wickerwork in a sleek sofa, set into a coffee-table or used as a Japanese-inspired lamp shade, rattan is proving an attractive and highly flexible home-decor accent. From Pataya Furniture Collection, Bangkok.

Above: A wicker inset works in a low table, complementing a "Zen-style" sitting room from Pataya Furniture Collection, Bangkok.

Previous Page: No longer relegated to the poolside patio, rattan offers both elegance and comfort (the natural fibres encourage ventilation) to these formal dining chairs from Pataya. The Pataya dining table is inlaid with rattan.

Reed Music

Queen Saowabha, the favourite consort of King Chulalongkorn, reportedly fell in love with the lilac-flowered water hyacinth *(Eichhornia crassipes)* on a visit to Yogyakarta, Indonesia. She planted the prolific river reed in the *khlongs* of Bangkok, which it proceeded to clog at an alarming rate. Another readily available weaving material—and an incentive to use it—was thus introduced to Thailand.

In recent years, a number of companies have sprung up to tap into the supply of this durable reed. Modern manufacturers cultivate the plant for a period of three months and only the stems are used. After they have been sun dried for five days, 30-m-long strips are woven into the desired shapes. High in flexibility and long-lasting, the stems do not require any kind of chemical treatment as water hyacinth is not prone to insects.

Approaching mandatory status in the indoor-outdoor tropical houses of the rich and famous, water hyacinth furniture comes in a range of natural colours (from dark to extremely light) and applications.

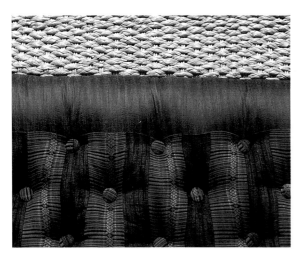

Top: The languid lines of this water-hyacinth deck-chair from Hangdong Rattan, Chiang Mai, look good on any terrace, especially if it overlooks endless rice paddies, as in Savas Ratakunjara's home.

Above and Far Right: Perfect for the poolside: a daybed in water hyacinth, inspired by the graceful bases of Thai temple architecture; and a silk-cotton mattress with a pattern from Nan province. Sop Moei Arts, Chiang Mai.

Above: Inside or outside, the water-hyacinth sofa upholstered in neutral-toned natural fabric is *de rigeur* in most tropical designer homes. In the home of Sawas Ratakunjara, this Hangdong version sits well with an antique water pot from Ratchaburi province and cushions trimmed with cowrie shells, probably inspired from designs from Naga House.

Above: With the idea for the cylindrical headrest taken from a rolled-up opium mat, this natural-coloured water-hyacinth daybed by Yothaka Int'l Co. Ltd has a cane frame. Yothaka exports its modern pieces to Europe and the USA (as well as in Asia) to such well known designers as Alberto Pinto, Jacques Garcia, Christian Liaigre and Gisela Trigano in France. Nancy Corzine of C & C Imports Inc. in the USA is a keen supporter; she, in turn, is a supplier of fabrics and furniture to the White House. Harrods in the UK stock some pieces and Club Med in Phuket and Bora-Bora and Banyan Tree Phuket, use water hyacinth furniture for both its texture and durability.

Opposite: In the cosy Bangkok townhouse of furniture designer Suwan Kongkhunthian, of Yothaka Int'l Co., Ltd, one of his arm-chairs, woven from dark–coloured water hyacinth with a dark-stained teak frame, is a focal point, com-plementing other natural highlights such as the stoneware-topped coffee-table (also designed by Suwan) and the jute mat.

Shooting Star

Once considered "the poor man's timber", bamboo is the commonest craft material in Thailand, traditionally used for everything from buckets to baskets, kitchen utensils to fish-traps.

At the turn of the century, the prestigious design house Chippendale and 150 other London producers were using bamboo as a raw material because of its immense strength and lightness. However, it was not until after the 1970s that interior designers such as Bali-based Linda Garland (whose clients include Richard Branson, David Bowie, Mick Jagger, Barry Humphries and Ringo Starr) made it acceptable for furnishings—mainly for holiday villas and hotels.

In the past few years, Thai designers have started to develop their own take on bamboo for items as diverse as upmarket dining- and living-room furniture and accessories such as vases, trays and paper products. With the same skill involved in picking individual stalks to be used for a *khit* bamboo basket or mat, the bamboo furniture craftsman must select his raw material in terms of straightness, thickness, colour and height. Once the piece is assembled, it is treated against parasites, hand-dowelled and polished until it becomes a unique work of art in itself.

The fastest growing plant on earth also answers modern architectural and design concerns about the need for sustainable raw materials. It looks great, too.

Opposite: From mat to coffee-table, chair to sofa, the modern applications of Thailand's most common craft material seem endless. From Gerard Collection, Chiang Mai.

Left: A close-up of the aquarium used as a novel lamp base as seen in the main picture, opposite.

Above: Bamboo dining chairs with tall backs and wicker seats and dining table from Gerard Collection photographed on the riverside deck at Baan Suan restaurant, Chiang Mai.

Below: An assortment of bamboo and rattan grain-storage baskets woven by Karen villagers in Ratchaburi province.

Right: Cane and gable. The juxtaposition of a late-Ayuthaya era temple gable with a plain white wooden triangle is a dramatic wall feature in Bangkok bamboo furniture shop Phen Siam. Wooden temple pillars, a Buddha shrine, reproduction terracotta horses and hemp cushions from Cocoon, complement the bamboo lounge suite.

Opposite: Southern style. *Yafaek* (grass) cushions from Surat Thani and *kachud* (water-reed) cushions and mat from Songkhla are great for lounging on the verandah while sipping tea from a *khantoke* (bowl tray). The round basket with a horse design is used in spirits-appeasing ceremonies by the Lao Song minority in Thailand.

Above: A rattan chair derived from an elephant seat (howdah) reflects the Pwo Karens' traditional form of transport. From Sop Moei Arts, Chiang Mai.

Above Right: Classic rattan chairs in a colonial design that was popular with expatriates who lived in many of the remaining colonial-style houses in the '60s and '70s at Naga House, Bangkok.

Right: This *kachud* (water-reed) mat made by Muslim villagers in southern Thailand exemplifies the intricacy of their patterns.

Opposite: Rattan and teak offer contemporary chic to these poolside chairs in the riverside house of Chulathat Kitibutr in Chiang Mai.

Left: An armchair in rattan and teak adds sophisticated comfort to a rustic *sala* in the same home.

Below: Rattan and teak chair and accompanying stool by the pool of Spa Palasthira's Bangkok home. From Thaipatana Furniture, Bangkok.

Far Left: The dramatic bedroom of fabric and fashion designer Nagara Sambandaraksa features a rolled antique opium-mat bedbase, an inverted temple gable, one of his trademark tie-dyed silk robes and a painting by Thai artist Thawan Duchanee.

Left: Antique lacquer tray from the Northeast on a reproduction opium mat from Gerard Collection.

Below: An antique opium mat is inlaid in the top of this desk by Bangkok furniture designer Prinya.

Earthenware
and Ceramics

Earth, water, fire, wood and metal: the five natural forces revered in the
East are all recruited to make ceramics. Because of this, it is believed
throughout Asia that these forces are endowed with supernatural
powers. Spanning Ban Chiang to bencharong, stoneware to celadon,
Thailand's earthenware and ceramics reflect not only the highest
levels of skill and the religious desire to earn merit, but the capacity
to absorb other cultures' styles while still remaining distinctly Thai.

Right: Two of these celadon water jars from Mae Rim Ceramics, Chiang Mai, show a stylised palm-leaf pattern popular with Japanese customers. Pink Heliconia and ginger complement the classic jade-green hue.

Previous page: Handsome tableware from Bangkok-based Earth & Fire is designed by Eakrit Praditsuwana.

Going Green

Celadon is a type of high fired stoneware with a wood-ash glaze ranging in colour from green to blue to grey. Reputed to possess magical and healing properties, celadons have long been prized in the East. Medicine prepared or stored in a celadon vessel was thought to be more potent. Imported Thai and Chinese celadons in Borneo and the Philippines were even given names and ranks and used as talismans to protect households.

Celadon production originated in China where it reached a peak in the Sung, Yuan and Ming Dynasties (10th–17th centuries). However, the technique of wood-ash glazing probably began more than 2,000 years ago during the Shang Dynasty when ash from wood-burning kilns landed on pottery which was being fired, producing a luminous, transparent glaze with a soft, slightly soapy feel. Other countries that are famed for the quality of their celadon ware include Korea and Japan where the craft was further developed.

Although Chinese celadon had been imported to Siam since Khmer times, Thai potters first started making celadon at Sukhothai and Sawankhalok in the 1300s and later in the Kingdom of Lanna. Here the art survived after the 16th century when wars and forced migrations caused the closure of the kilns elsewhere.

Clockwise from Top: Modern celadons from Living Space, Chiang Mai, serve as jewellery containers, one topped with a pewter lotus-bud lid, on a dressing table; bathroom accessories including a pewter-capped burner which doubles as a pot-pourri holder; and vases on a mantelpiece. Traditionally, the antique mirror on the dressing table would have been placed on the floor or on a low pedestal and its high-class owner would kneel or sit on a cushion or mat in front of it. Living Space is famed for its especially light-coloured, almost white, celadons, often embossed with leaf or insect motifs set beneath the glaze.

Right: Silver *nagas* (semi-divine cobras which can assume human form in Buddhist mythology) from Naga House, Bangkok, embrace Thai silk napkins.

Below: Like folds of silk ribbon at a racing contest, glossy green banana leaves, interspersed with white tree flowers, superbly set off a Thai lacquered offering tray.

Below Right: Crown flowers *(Calotropis gigantea),* which incidentally inspired the Thai Airways International logo, adorn floral arrangements called *phoum.* Their rounded pyramidal shape resembles a budding lotus.

After World War II, the tradition was revived and now there are several kilns producing quality celadon. Ewers, dishes, bowls with lids, and bottles with two small loop handles at the neck are common items.

Requiring very carefully controlled, reduction-firing conditions and a smoky flame reaching temperatures of more than 1,200°C, the celadon glaze consists of one to three per cent iron, ground minerals, wood ash and paddy clay. Too much oxygen yields shades varying from olive green through yellow to brown. Other kinds of ash, such as those from rice or bean stalks or bamboo, and other clays also vary the glaze colour. If the kiln does not reach the critical temperature the piece remains opaque.

The ware was not known as "celadon" until the last years of the 19th century when the term was commonly used to name the grey-green colour of a costume worn by the shepherd Celadon in the 17th-century French play, *L'Astrée,* by Honoré d'Urfe.

Left: Celadon and silver are timeless statements of style, here underlined by a northeast Thai silk *ikat (mat mee)* table runner, cutlery with mother-of-pearl handles from Maya Ethnic Craft, Bangkok, and blue trumpet vine flowers. The modern flatware is from Sansai Celadon, Chiang Mai. The silver napkin holders are antique betelnut-leaf containers.

Modern copies of Ayuthaya-period bencharong show *thepanom*, a minor Buddhist deity *(left)*, and *rajasingh*, the royal lion *(below left)*. Other traditional Thai designs on Sino-Siamese ceramics include *norasingh* (half-man, half-lion minor gods), Garuda (Vishnu's part-eagle, part-man steed), *kinnaras* (half-bird, half-man creatures) and mythical animals, mostly of Indian origin, plus Chinese floral and fire motifs.

Rainbow Ware

More than any other ceramic, bencharong reflects the Thais' exuberant love of colour and flamboyant decoration. This may stem from their intrinsic sense of ceremony and fun, as well as from the extravagant beauty of their natural environment.

Traditional Thai art generally uses more hues and patterns than that of most cultures and some bencharong pieces may seem a little garish to foreigners (even the Chinese, who made bencharong specifically for the Thais, did not consider it worthy enough for their own use). However, most are stunning not only for their beauty but as vibrant historical records.

The word bencharong comes from the Sanskrit words *panch* (five) and *rang* (coloured, as well as pleasing). To the Thais, the number five has magical connotations associated with the five elements important in Hindu-Buddhist religions.

In the 14th century, Thai potters were making a crude form of bencharong but the upper classes soon turned to the Chinese for a more high-quality version. Coloured enamels were added over the glaze in a descending scale of temperatures to fuse them to the surface. A later form called lai nam thong (gold-washed) was strictly reserved for royalty.

Production peaked after Bangkok became the capital in 1782 and stopped in 1910 with the collapse of the Ching Dynasty. In the past few decades, this distinctive ware has been locally resurrected with stunning results.

Top: History in the making. Nagara Sambandaraksa's private antique bencharong collection includes ancient shapes such as bowls, cups, *toh prik* (small covered) jars once used for cosmetics or medicines and *toh* (large covered) jars for sauces, soups, syrups and holy water. Most of the jars have stupa or lotus-bud finials and shapes of Indian, Chinese or Khmer origin.

Left: A modern interpretation of bencharong, from Naga House, in a Western-style table setting, at Nagara's home.

Traditional Ceramics

"The King has eight or 10 stone houses of wealth inconceivable. In some are urns full of ticuls and gold dust; others are full of Japanese swords. There are even pieces of porcelain which cannot contain poison without breaking."
—Nicolas Gervais, 1683

This reference by a visiting Frenchman to King Narai the Great of Ayuthaya reveals not only the delicacy of his porcelain collection but the belief that a celadon container would change hue or crack if it came into contact with poisoned food. Such was the mystique and reverence surrounding ceramics in Siam, where they were reserved mainly for royalty and the ruling classes.

Earthenware vessels, including beautiful red-and-white painted pottery, had been produced by a sophisticated culture from 3,600BC to 200AD in Ban Chiang in northeast Thailand. These prehistoric people also wove textiles and produced some of Asia's earliest bronze and copper tools. Ceramics continued to be fired in the

Opposite, Top: Glazed water droppers in the form of hunchback figures (Sawankhalok, c. 16th century).

Opposite Middle Left: Fish motifs painted directly underneath the glaze began in the Sukhothai kilns and continued, with stylistic variations such as the floral and tendril design on this plate (c. 15th–16th century), at Sawankhalok.

Opposite, Bottom Left: Modern reproductions of Sukhothai plates show Chinese-influenced fish motifs.

Opposite, Bottom Right: A 16th-century *kendi* (water jar) with a Sawankhalok-style breast-like spout.

Above: Sawankhalok covered boxes (c. 16th century) for storing cosmetics, medicines, spices and betel-chewing equipment. The one on the right resembles a mangosteen; the others Indian reliquary urns with "lotus-bud" handles.

Far Left and Left: These hand-made reproduction pieces have an embossed buff-coloured pattern typical of the Sukhothai era.

open air in the centuries which followed. The Buddhist Mon people of the Dvaravati Kingdom (7th–10th century), congregated in the Chao Phraya Valley, created ash-glazed, wheel-turned earthenware and unglazed terracotta. They were absorbed in the 11th and 12th centuries by the Khmer Empire, which built kilns to fire glazed wares.

The Thai Kingdom of Sukhothai (1238–1368), established after Mon settlers from southeast China revolted against their Khmer overlords, is also remembered for its glazed ceramics. They were made in kilns first in the city of Sukhothai in the early 14th century—probably with the help of Chinese potters—and then in the Sawankhalok area of the satellite city of Si Satchanlai.

The indigenous craft or *chang* continued at Sawankhalok even after the Kingdom of Ayuthaya (1350–1767) gained sovereignty over Sukhothai in the late 14th century. Thai ceramics, in many glaze colours including celadon, became a thriving export to other Southeast Asian countries and Japan, while Chinese, Vietnamese and Japanese ceramics were imported to Thailand. Shapes and patterns were influenced by India, Sri Lanka, China and the Khmers. The Sawankhalok kilns closed in the 16th century after raids by the northern Lanna kingdom. It was not until the 18th century that Thai motifs reappeared on ceramics in Thailand, through the import of over-glazed enamel wares called bencharong and lai nam thong from China. These Sino-Thai ceramics were specifically designed for the Thai market during the Ratanakosin period (1782–1910) after Ayuthaya fell to the Burmese.

Imports of bencharong ceased in 1910 but since World War II, several Thai companies have started making it locally. Other producers are making glazed stoneware, including celadon, similar to that made in the kilns of Sukhothai and Sawankhalok, as well as terracotta and stucco sculptures first seen in Thailand during Mon and Khmer times.

Far Left: Far from jaded. Using traditional methods and materials, Mengrai Kilns, based in Chiang Mai, produces handmade stonewares in exciting shades, including the latest red, purple and blue, using different glaze ingredients and firing temperatures. These highly coloured pots have an appealing reflective sheen, whereas the more traditional green ware are more opaque.

Left: Shades of the past. Among Mengrai's classic celadon range, each piece of which takes about six weeks to make, are characteristic Sawankhalok shapes such as "eared" jugs which traditionally contained condiments or lustral water. A string was looped through the "ears" or rings on the neck, allowing it to be hung out of the reach of insects.

Mon Days

The Mons were an ethnic group who originally migrated from southern China to establish the Dvaravati kingdom in Thailand and lower Burma from the seventh century. After the kingdom was conquered by the Khmers in the 11th century a small Mon power base called Haripunjaya remained dominant in northern Thailand until the 13th century.

Although they borrowed Indian and Sri Lankan forms for some of their stoneware, such as stupa and pumpkin shapes, this Buddhist people created some of Southeast Asia's first sculptures. The Mons' terracotta figures, stucco bas-reliefs and glazed architectural ceramics were particularly exceptional.

The Mon continue to live throughout Thailand, particularly in areas like Pra-Pradaeng, Ratchaburi and Sukhothai, but now they are totally assimilated with the Thai culture. One Mon village in particular, situated on an island called Koh Kred in the Chao Phraya River 30 minutes by boat from Bangkok, is famous for its thriving cottage industry of potters. The local clay is particularly good for fashioning water jars and pots that make strong statements in the garden.

Left: These water coolers made in Koh Kred, two of which have three parts (lid, body and base), replicate traditional Mon forms.

Right: National treasure Khun Yai ("Grandmother Tee") made these terracotta water containers in present-day Sukhothai. Featuring her trademark "rooster" lids, they have the waisted stems and "pumpkin" forms typical of Mon earthenware vessels.

Tropical Trappings

Thai-style decorating is not relegated to interiors. The gardens of royal palaces and Buddhist monasteries were deliberately designed for pleasure and peace respectively. More recently, with the burgeoning interest in landscaping, designers are turning to the country's natural luxuriance and craft traditions to create some of the world's best tropical gardens. The trend applies not only to five-star resorts in sweeping grounds but minute metropolitan balconies and courtyards.

Sukhothai architects, like their Mon and Khmer predecessors, used stucco extensively for decoration but only for religious structures as the use of durable materials for other buildings was forbidden. Demons, dwarfs, mythical animals and divinities enlivened the architecture of Buddhist temples and monuments and reminded worshippers of Buddhist mythology.

Old or reproduction statuary and bas-reliefs originally of religious significance, and water jars and pots traditionally of a utilitarian nature, today lend an exotic authenticity to outside spaces. Landscape designers throughout Asia are tapping into the potential of moss-and-fern-gathering goddesses and lichen-imbued stone panels. Bas-reliefs and statues from companies such as Ban Phor Liang Meun in Chiang Mai are now hot items for the green-fingered. The texture and colour of the terracotta quickly takes on an attractive patina, so that a few years after inception, the stoneware looks as if it has been there forever.

Above and Right: Lush living. Old or reproduction water jars such as these are focal points unadorned, or when planted with lotuses, lilies or other water flora evocative of Eastern water gardens.

Opposite Above: The "drip" design on this contemporary water jar crafted at Doi Din Daeng kilns by Somluk Pantiboon, an award-winning Chiang Rai born artist who trained in Japan, recalls the days when poor glaze quality caused it to flow down the pot as it vitrified.

Left: This carved and glazed reproduction lotus jar from Tao Hong Tai in Ratchaburi province, displayed in Nagara's garden, displays a distinct Chinese influence in motifs and shape.

Far Left: Pot luck. The octagonal shape of this glazed lotus jar from Ratchaburi province is thought to be auspicious in Thailand and other Asian countries.

Right: A terracotta reproduction of a worshipping deity from Wat Chedi Ched Yod, Chiang Mai, looks at home in this natural niche. Inspired by designs at Khmer temples in Cambodia and Northeastern Thailand, Suttipong and Maliwan Maiyun at Chiang Mai's Ban Phor Liang Meun specialise in reproducing such ancient forms and bas-reliefs, in order to reintroduce a sense of mystery and atmosphere into modern-day gardens.

Above Right: A detail of a lintel showing an *apasara* (Thai court lady) has been placed in a garden where ferns and other foliage have been encouraged to grow around it. Such items add a feeling of exoticism in small plots.

Above Far Right: Bird of paradise. This terracotta reproduction of a guardian Garuda from Ban Phor Liang Meun, Chiang Mai, is inspired by a Khmer version at Banteay Srei temple, Angkor.

Right: A Lanna-style *kinnari* (half-bird, half-woman figure) guards a *kala* (demon face representing time, used by the Khmers and Mons) arch under which an *apasara* resides.

Left: Story in stone. A terracotta bas-relief depicts a scene from the *Ramakian*, the Thai version of the famous Indian epic *Ramayana*, at the Regent Hotel, Chiang Mai.

Below Left: Thai *apasaras* (court ladies) grace this bas-relief from Ban Phor Liang Muen, Chiang Mai. This company has revived the use of terracotta in decorative motifs with styles not only from Thailand but from India, Cambodia, Indonesia, China and Myanmar in recent years.

Right: This Khmer-style bas-relief showing a king and his army going to war makes a stunning wall feature in Nagara Sambandaraksa's garden.

Romantic
Thai Nights

From Bangkok to Brussels, residences to restaurants, candles are one of the hottest decor items today. Recreate the romance of a languid Lanna night by floating them with flowers in a pool or suspending them from the ceiling of an open-air *sala*. Make light of the situation by using gilded coconut shells or celadon sauce-bowls as bases or make your own wind-proof lanterns with rice paper. Colours, shapes and sizes vary as much as the floral arrangements which are natural complements. From elaborate hand-carved affairs traditionally used for Buddhist Lent to simple wicks set in terracotta, Thai-style candles are creating more than a flicker of interest inside and outside the home.

Festive Flowers

From daily religious gestures such as lighting a candle or offering a lotus bloom at a shrine to national and local holidays, celebrating is a way of life for the Thais.

Songkran, a religious holiday marking the Buddhist New Year, is a major three-day event in mid-April blending reverent ritual and riotous fun. Statues of Buddha are symbolically bathed and passers-by copiously splashed; homes are spring-cleaned and adorned with *malai* (garlands) and other floral decorations.

For wedding ceremonies, the entrances of houses and temples are arched with "wedding gates" crafted from banana leaves and coconut branches, while the windows are festooned with traditional flower displays made of crown or "love flowers" *(dok rak)*. Even babies' cradles are draped with fragrant flower mobiles made of jasmine, a symbol of purity, to encourage sleep.

The traditional Thai art of floral arranging (*bai-sri*), which originated in the women's sector of the royal court, requires much skill and training. One type of rounded, pagoda-shaped arrangement, called *phoum*, is made by sticking multicoloured flowers into a wet core of earth, sawdust or sand; others, called *bai-sri pak cham*, are made of banana-leaf cones capped with jasmine flowers and sometimes salty eggs.

The resulting masterpieces are used mainly for religious offerings in ceremonies ranging from the consecration of spirit houses to the "festival of lights", Loi Krathong. In a country of such verdant beauty, it is only natural to incorporate flowers and foliage in one's living spaces.

Above: Malai (garlands) are made of rose petals, lady of the night leaves and crown flowers, threaded thickly together. Highly complex versions that require many hours of work are used to greet royalty and high ranking foreign guests, but in the above case a specially long garland is used for decorating the reception area of a private home. Nearly everyone who visits a shrine brings a *malai* as an offering to the resident spirit and Buddhist altars in Thai houses receive a fresh *malai* daily.

Page 130: Follow the yellow-lit road. Terracotta bowls filled with candles create a wonderland of lights at Sri Deva Giri ("God's prosperous hill"), Chiang Mai.

Left: Frond welcome. An arch of banana leaves and coconut branches frames raw cotton lanterns outside the northern style home of Diether and Susie Von Boehm-Bezing. This type of arch is a typical Lanna decoration, freshly constructed at gateways leading to the house to welcome guests during festive occasions.

Far Left: Hanging *malai* made of crown flowers is traditionally hung in windows as a decoration during wedding ceremonies or at the ordination ceremony of a male member of the family entering the monkhood.

Floating Dreams

Legend has it that during a court picnic in the 12th lunar month of the Thai calendar while the country was flooded during the rainy season, a beautiful and learned court lady named Lady Nophamat, introduced a new *krathong* to King Pra Ruang, ruler of Sukhothai. In the shape of a lotus flower, it was placed on the river for the king's enjoyment and thus the custom of Loi Krathong ("to float leaf cups") began.

Others say that the loveliest of Thai festivals honours Mae Khongkha, the Mother or Goddess of Waters. Leaf cups *(krathong)* made of banana leaves and lotus flowers carrying candles, incense sticks and lotus blossoms are painstakingly assembled, then set adrift in ponds and waterways. They are often snatched a short while later by children looking for the coins which are also traditionally placed in the centre of the *krathong*.

One does not have to wait for a full moon to celebrate with floating flowers and candles. While the brightly coloured blossoms of hibiscus, plumeria, lotus, jasmine and chrysanthemums are traditionally used by the Thais, almost any flower is suitable, as long as it is cut and placed in a pool or pot at the last moment (orchids last the longest). Whether the occasion is an elegant wedding reception for 300 around a tropical resort's infinity edge pool or an informal barbecue in your own backyard (don't forget to grill your fish whole, Thai-style), the combination of fire, flowers and water adds sizzle and sparkle.

Above: The classic *krathong* is formed from banana leaves folded into the shape of an open lotus and mounted on a slice of banana stalk. Incense, candles and pink lotus blooms adorn the middle.

Right and Far Right: Other *krathong* exemplify *bai-sri* arrangements with cones of banana leaves capped by jasmine crowns.

Above: Buoyant mood. Yellow chrysanthemums and pink orchids adorn urns and the swimming-pool at the Regent Resort, Chiang Mai.

Far Left: Candles in the wind. Simple floating tea lights amid bouganvillea and plumeria blooms make for an enchanted evening.

Left: Swan lake. A classic *krathong* glides with the grace of a white water bird.

The Light Fantastic

An Eastern symbol for spiritual insight and meditation, the candle flame continues to entrance man with a lure unrivalled by even the most sophisticated modern lighting. This may be due to some primeval attachment to the life-giving properties of fire or simply because of the romance and other-worldliness evoked by a subtle flickering light. Whatever the cause for this moth-like attraction, candles are hotter than they have ever been in the style world.

In Thailand, the art of candle carving has religious connotations. The beginning of Buddhist Lent (Phansa) is observed by the Candle Festival when thousands of carved candles, some several metres high, are paraded along the streets and presented to local temples.

From elaborate hand-carved affairs to versions fragranced with exotic oils such as sandalwood or natural insect repellants such as citronella, the wide choice of candles is matched by ways to display them. Almost anything can be used as a candleholder, from an antique offering tray to a terracotta dish, a celadon

Far Left: The courtyard at Sri Deva Giri, Chiang Mai, glimmers like a glow-worm grotto.

Left: On the table in the reception *sala* of Sri Deva Giri, reproductions of temple woodcarvings and (at front) Balinese ceramics are striking candleholders. Celadon candleholders shaped like typical Thai sauce bowls are in niches at the ends of each sofa. An Ayuthaya-era temple bell makes a stunning backdrop.

Top: Old flame. A gold and red lacquered antique Lanna offering tray makes an unusual candlebase.

Above: Candles on gilded bamboo are combined with strings of jasmine flowers and dried palm leaves.

sauce bowl to a coconut shell. Suspended from the ceiling, placed on a coffee- or dining-table, nestled in a niche or an empty fireplace, or scattered like glow-worms throughout a garden in tiny terracotta pots *(tien prateep)* or on bamboo or rattan supports, candles create a sense of ceremony and magic, indoors and out.

The pool party in particular lends itself to decorating with candles. For the function at a Bangkok home shown opposite—where the Ambassador of Italy, H.E. Mario Piersigilli and wife Enza, and the Conductor of the chamber orchestra I Musici mingled with such Thai dignatories as the Permanent Secretary of Foreign Affairs of the Thai Government Nitti Pibulsongkram—wire mesh was folded into cylinders and covered with white, translucent rice paper to make wind-proof lanterns. The result was a lovely soft, diffused glow around the whole arena. Fresh white lotuses were incorporated into the design for a truly Asian accent. The lanterns were suspended from the eaves of the *sala* and positioned by the pool to maximise their reflections in the water. As one attendee recollected, the atmosphere was truly magical.

Far Left and Left: A flare for entertaining. Specially designed paper lanterns are suspended from the *sala* and placed around the edge of Spa Palasthira's Bangkok pool. White lotuses, green lotus-seed pods and lotus leaves decorate the buffet table. Styled by Sakul Intakul Studio, Bangkok.

Top and Above: Trunk call. These striking candles from Lots of Style, Bangkok feature terracotta and hand-carved elephants.

Left: The entrance to the guesthouse at Sri Deva Giri, Chiang Mai.

Below, Clockwise from Top Left: In a nutshell. A citronella candle in a coconut shell rests on a bamboo support; candles flicker in glass cones surrounded by rattan from Oriental Style, Chiang Mai; a coconut husk (with the inside of the shell gilded) makes a rustic candle holder; gilded coconut shells impart a golden glow. The last two are from Nawaporn, Bangkok.

Above: Fancy floorwork. Traditional Lanna terracotta candle bases called *tien prateep* and coconut shells punctuate the path and bridge across this reflecting carp pond in Chiang Mai.

Acknowledgments

AKA,
19 Rama 9 Rd., Suanluang,
Bangkok 10250.
Tel (66-2) 300-5131–4
Fax (66-2) 300-5559
Email sivika@eggthai.com
http://www.eggthai.com

Baan Suan Restaurant,
25 Moo 3 San-Phi-Sua, Muang,
Chiang Mai 50300.
Tel (66-53) 854-169-70, 852-751
Fax (66-53) 854-171

Ban Phor Liang Meun's Terracotta Arts,
36 Prapokklao Rd. Soi 2, Muang,
Chiang Mai 50200.
Tel (66-53) 278-187, 277-463
Fax (66-53) 275-895

Cocoon Design Co. Ltd,
999 Gaysorn Plaza, 3rd Floor,
Room 3-03, Ploenchit Rd., Lumpini,
Phatumvan, Bangkok 10330.
Tel (66-2) 656-1006
Fax (66-2) 656-1007

Earth & Fire Co. Ltd.,
19 Rama 9 Rd., Suanluang,
Bangkok 10250.
Tel (66-2) 300-5131-4
Fax (66-2) 300-5559
Email earth-fire@thai.com

Fai Ngam,
Apartment E. Nimanhaemin Rd.,
Soi 1, Muang, Chiang Mai 50200.
Tel/Fax (66-53) 895-012, 221-130
ext Apt. E.

Gerard Collection Co. Ltd.,
6/23–24 Nimmanhaemin Rd.,
Chiang Mai 50200.
Tel (66-53) 220-604
Fax (66-53) 216-567
Email bambu@chmai.loxinfo.co.th
http://www.ThaiBamboo.com

Gong Dee Gallery,
17/3 Mu 13., T. Sankamphang,
A. Sankamphang, Chiang Mai 50130.
Tel (66-53) 332-783, 392-428, 392-733
Fax (66-53) 331 783
Showroom:
10, 12 Soi 1, Nimanhemin Rd.,
Suthep, Muang, Chiang Mai 50000.
Tel (66-53) 225-032, 219-499
Fax (66-53) 215-768

Hangdong Rattan,
54, 56 Kamphangdin Rd., Changklan,
Chiang Mai 50100.
Tel (66-53) 208-167
Fax (66-53) 275-735

Jim Thompson,
9 Surawong Rd., Bangkok 10500.
Tel (66-2) 632-8100
Fax (66-2) 236-6777
Email office@jimthompson.com

K/J,
181/41, Chotananiwet 2, Moo 3,
Chiang Mai 50300.
Tel (66-53) 218-495
Fax (66-53) 218-496
Email soik@usa.net

Khomapastr Ltd. Part,
56–58 Nares Rd., Siphaya Bangrak,
Bangkok 10500.
Tel (66-2) 266-8415, 234-1460
Fax (66-2) 237-0802
River City Showroom:
23 Trok Rongnamkaeng, Yota Rd.,
Sampantawong, Bangkok 10100.
Tel (66-2) 267-7727

Kingdom of Father Ceramic,
Gaysorn Plaza, 2nd floor, Rajdamri Rd.,
Bangkok 10330.
Tel (66-2) 656-1316

Living Space Co. Ltd.,
276–278, Thaphae Rd., T. Chang Moi, A.
Muang, Chiang Mai 50300.
Tel (66-53) 874-299 Fax (66-53) 874-310
Email livingsp@loxinfo.co.th

Lots of Style Co. Ltd. "Candles of Love",
946/6 Thonglor 20, Sukhumvit 55,
Bangkok 10110.
Tel (66-2) 714-9486

Lotus,
32/9–10, Soi Veeratos, Sukhumvit 21,
Klong Toey, Bangkok 10110.
Tel (66-2) 258-0470, 258-3668,
258-3669
Fax (66-2) 259-1702
Email jvbkk@asiaacess.net.th

Mae Rim Ceramic Studio,
165 M 8, Donkaew, Maerim,
Chiang Mai 50180.
Tel (66-53) 214-676
Fax (66-53) 210-156
Email maerimceramic@hotmail.com

Maya Ethnic Craft,
Room 26–29/1, 2nd Floor, Gaysorn
Plaza, Ploenchit Road, Bangkok 10330.
Tel (66-2) 656-1793

Mengrai Kilns R.O.P.,
79/2 Arak Rd, T. Phrasingh A.
Muang, Chiang Mai 50200.
Tel (66-53) 272-063, 814-080
Fax (66-53) 815-017, 278-676
Email mengraik@loxinfo.co.th
P.O. Box 37 Phrasingh,
Chiang Mai 50200.

Naga House,
315 Soi Ongkarak, Samsen Rd. 28, Dusit,
Bangkok 10300.
Tel (66-2) 669-3416-8, 669-3493-4
Fax (66-2) 669-3377
Email naga@ksc.th.com

Nawaporn,
2nd Floor, Gaysorn Plaza,
Bangkok 10330.
Tel (66-2) 656-1100

N. V. Aranyik Company Ltd.,
48/3 Moo 5, Tambon Maela Amphur
Nakornluang, Ayuthaya 13260.
Tel (66-35) 359-657-8, 285-319
Fax (66-35) 359-282
Email n_v_aranyik@aranyik.com

Oriental Style Products Co. Ltd.,
36 Charoenrat Rd., Chiang Mai 50000.
Tel (66-53) 245-724, 243-156
Fax (66-53) 245-725
Email oriental@loxinfo.co.th

Pataya Furniture Collection,
753–755 Sukhumvit Rd.,
North-Klongton, Wadhana,
Bangkok 10110.
Tel (66-2) 258-7280, 259-8095
Fax (66-2) 259-8094

**Paya Handwoven Fabrics and Accessories
for the Home,**
961 Sukhumvit Road
(between Soi 51 & 53),
Bangkok 10110.
Tel (66-2) 259-2041, 662-4026
Fax (66-2) 259-2041
Email payashop@yahoo.com

Phen Siam,
3rd Floor, Gaysorn Plaza, Bangkok 10330.
Tel/Fax (66-2) 656-1148

Pure Design Concepts Co. Ltd.,
30 Ruam Rudee Road, Bangkok 10330.
Tel (66-2) 253-1719 Fax (66-2) 255-8279

Sansai Celadon,
160 Moo 13 Tambon Pa Phai,
Sansai, Chiang Mai 50210.
Tel (66-53) 496-412 Fax (66-53) 498-413

Sop Moei Arts,
Bangkok Showroom:
Sukhumvit Soi 49 Soi Promsri I
(Soi Klang Racket Club Compound)
Bangkok 10110.
Tel (66-2) 712-8039

Chiang Mai Showroom:
The Elephant Quay House, 31–35
Chareonrajd Rd., Chiang Mai 50000.
Tel/Fax (66-53) 260-844
Email linnea@sopmoeiarts.com

Tamnan Mingmuang,
3rd Floor, Thaniya Plaza (opposite
The Legend), Silom Rd.,
Bangkok 10500.
Tel (66-2) 231-2120, 231-2139
Fax (66-2) 231-2139

Thaipatana Furniture,
761 Near Soi 41–43,
Sukhumvit Rd., Bangkok 10110.
Tel (66-2) 258-4724, 259-3561
Fax (66-2) 261-6547

The Peninsula Bangkok,
333 Charoennakorn Rd., Klongsarn,
Bangkok 10600.
Tel (66-2) 861-2888, 861-1111
Fax (66-2) 861-1112
Email pbk@peninsula.com

The Lanna Spa, The Regent Resort,
Chiang Mai 502, Moo 1,
Mae Rim-Samoeng Old Rd., Mae Rim,
Chiang Mai 50180.
Tel (66-53) 298-181
Fax (66-53) 291-189
Email rcm.reservations@fourseasons.com

Vila Cini,
30, 32, 34 Charoenrat Rd.,
Chiang Mai 50000.
Tel (66-53) 244-025, 244-780
Fax (66-53) 244-867

Yothaka Int'l Co. Ltd.,
3rd Floor, 1028/5 Rama 4 Rd.,
Thungmahamek, Sathorn,
Bangkok 10120.
Tel (66-2) 679-8631, 679-8632
Fax (66-2) 679-8965
Email yothaka@cscoms.com

Connect